MAO—
A YOUNG MAN FROM
THE YANGTZE VALLEY

MAO—
A YOUNG MAN FROM
THE YANGTZE VALLEY

by Bernadette P.N. Shih

Ashley books inc •
Box 768 · Port Washington, N. Y. 11050

Published simultaneously in Canada by George J. McLeod, Limited, 73 Bathurst Street, Toronto, Ontario M5V 2P8

MAO—A Young Man From The Yangtze Valley, © Copyright 1974 by Bernadette P.N. Shih

Library of Congress Number: 74-76433

ISBN: 0-87949-026-8

Address information to Ashley Books, Inc., Box 768, Port Washington, New York 11050

Published by Ashley Books, Inc.
Manufactured in the United States of America

First Edition

FOR MY PARENTS,
Anna, Eric and Bill

Contents

MAO—
A YOUNG MAN FROM THE YANGTZE VALLEY

The Capture of
Nanking by the
People's Liberation Army

A storm swept over Chungshan
Our mighty army, a million strong, crossed the Great
*   River.*
The City, a tiger crouching, a dragon curling, out-
*   shines its ancient glories;*
Heaven and earth have been overturned in heroic
*   triumph.*
We must use our power to pursue the tottering foe
And must not seek idle fame like the overlord
*   Hsiang Yu.*
If nature has feeling, it will
*   grow old and watch our seas turn into mulberry*
*   fields.*

Mao Tse-tung

Allow me to introduce myself. I am Ho Ch'ang-ch'eng*, fifth daughter of Ho Tzu-chen and Mao Jun-chih, better known to you as Mao Tse-tung which literally means Hair Enrich-east.

I adopted my mother's surname because my parents were divorced in 1947. My first name, Ch'ang-ch'eng, means "long journey," for I was born in Pao-an after the historic Long March which lasted from October, 1934 to October 1935 when Mother walked over six thousand miles in one year, across eleven provinces and eighteen mountain chains, from central China to northwestern China, with the People's Red Army.

Before 1927, members of the Communist Party of China, (founded in 1921), were admitted to the Nationalist Party which was founded by Sun Yat-sen in 1912. The Communists were the chief allies of the Nationalists during the Nationalist Revolu-

*Fictitious name. Other than the brief mention in Edgar Snow's *RED STAR OVER CHINA*, that a daughter was born to the Maos just before he left Pao-an, I could not substantiate from other published sources that there was indeed such a daughter. Most documented sources are of the opinion that the five daughters by Mao's third wife, Ho Tzu-chen, were left in the care of local peasants during the Long March and their whereabouts now are still unknown. But then Mr. Snow was there in Pao-an!

11

tion 1924 to 1927, when Chiang Kai-shek, the Nationalist leader led expeditions against the Northern Warlords of China in an attempt to unify the country. But in April of 1927, Chiang renounced the Nationalist-Communist alliance and executed many of the Communist leaders and forced the rest to go underground.

Some of the Communist leaders lived illegally in the coastal cities, while others, among them Father, escaped to the countrysides, where they organized peasant armies and set up small Communist-run principalities called 'Chinese Soviets'. The first such Chinese Soviet was established at Tsalin, in southeastern Hunan, Father's native province, in November 1927. Another Soviet was established in central Kiangsi in 1928, and shortly afterwards the movement spread into western Fukien. For a long time, the Nationalists denied the existence of these Chinese Soviets, and the Moscow-influenced Shanghai Communist Central Committee belittled the importance of their rivals' successes.

The official organ of the Comintern went so far as to spread rumors that Father had died of consumption!

By 1930, there were more than 1000 Soviet co-operatives in Kiangsi alone. And in February of the same year, a Provincial Soviet government was established—Kiangsi, under Father's leadership.

Several Red armies were in operation, based on the Soviet areas of central and southern China. From October 1927 to October 1937, Red armies found hiding places in high mountains. Father chose a range called Chingkanshan, with a circuit of about 150 miles, an area covered with a heavy growth of bamboos and evergreens. Mist hung over it most of the year. It was a natural fortress and refuge, with only five roads leading to it.

Generalissimo Chiang led five "annihilation campaigns" against these Soviets. During the fifth "annihilation campaign", which lasted from October 1933 to October 1934, Chiang mobilized over 900,000 troops against the Red armies in the Soviet districts. He had a much larger and superior army, and an expensive and distinguished staff of foreign military advisers at his disposal. To unbalance Chiang's superior army, Father's peasant army retreated when the enemy advanced. They harassed when the enemy escaped. They pursued when the enemy retreated. They attacked when the enemy were tired.

Chiang tried to encircle the Kiangsi Soviet, the main center of the Communists, with a blockade, and squeeze it to the death. But the Red Army, led by Father and General Chu Teh, managed to escape from complete encirclement, and thus they began the historic Long March to northwestern China.

13

During the March, Father and Chu Teh emerged as leaders. Chiang offered a quarter of a million silver dollars for their capture, dead or alive!

In January, 1935, three months after they started out from Kiangsi, the Red Army reached Tsunyi in Kweichow Province, where they halted for eleven days, their longest rest during the entire trip. As they had done at each of their stops, the women's propaganda corps and political workers immediately scattered to drum up support among the residents. Banks and warehouses were seized. Money and supplies from the seized banks and warehouses were handed out free, to the poor.

The brief respite at Tsunyi provided Father with an opportunity to hold a top-level conference of utmost significance, for it resulted in the decline of the Moscow-trained clique and the beginning of Father's dominance in the Chinese Communist Party. The Moscow faction of returned students, led by Li Li San, wanted to attack and hold large cities as future and safe bases. Father wanted to seek a base in the northwest from which to resist Japanese inroads into China. Father was elected General Secretary of the Party and the Central Committee and his tactical procedure was adopted unanimously.

Chiang did not believe the 85,000 men and 35 women Communist marchers would be able to cross the Yangtze River which blocked their way to the northwest. Even after crossing the Yangtze River at the border of Yunan Province, they would still have to cross the impassable Tatu, a turbulent branch of the Yangtze. When the marchers reached Yenan, Shensi Province in the northwest, their numbers had dwindled to 20,000. Of these, many were new recruits who had joined along the way.

When at long last the marchers found themselves safe at Wa Yao Pao, a little out-of-the-way village in Shensi in December of 1935, Father shouted to his followers in his heavy Hunanese accent: "The Long March we have just completed is the first of its kind ever recorded in human history. It is a manifesto of unconquerable force, a herald of the true Messiah, and a broadcaster of the seeds of revolution!"

During the March, the Red Army and their families were constantly pursued and bombed by the Chinese Nationalists, and if that weren't enough, everyone was plagued by lice!

Aside from having to endure a hectic and dangerous existence, Father had to fight for his political survival as well. But most of the time, he remained calm, unruffled and a good listener. In order to forget the sordid details of a day-to-day guerrilla existence, he wrote poetry.

Before crossing the gorges of the Upper Yangtze, he wrote:

Loushan Pass

Cold is the west wind,
Far in the frosty air the wild geese call in the
    dawn moonlight
In the dawn moonlight!
Horse hoofs ring sharp,
And the bugle's note is muted.
The strong pass is guarded with iron,
Yet this very day in one step we shall cross its
    summit.
We shall cross its summit!
Before us the hills are blue like the sea,
And the dying sun like blood.

At the end of the Long March in October 1935,
he wrote:

The Long March

The Red Army fears not the hardship of a long
    march,
One thousand mountains and ten thousand riv-
    ers are nothing.

The Wumeng peaks are like mounds beneath
    our feet.
And the five chains of mountains are no more
    than small waves.

16

The cliffs, burning and wreathed in clouds,
Are washed by the Gold Sand River.
Ice are the links of the Tatu River chain.
Soldiers fear not the snow of Minshan.
When the last pass is pushed through, the armies
    smiled.

Mother was pregnant with me then, and during one bombing raid, shrapnels struck her, inflicting sixteen wounds that caused her much pain. Yet, miraculously, she survived.

You might have already heard of me from Father's biographer, Mr. Edgar Snow, a journalist from the United States. Unfortunately, Mr. Snow passed away before he had a chance to revisit China with President Richard M. Nixon of the United States in February of 1972.

I was the healthy little baby girl Mr. Snow mentioned in his well-known book, *Red Star Over China,* when he talked very briefly about Mother.

As I look as far as I can into my memories, I recall four sets of caves, scattered around the Yenan hills of northwestern China, in which my family lived and worked between 1937 and 1947.

Strictly speaking, they were not really caves. Two of them were just separate structures of earth and stone built on cliffs; the other two were partly dug out of the hillsides, with rooms and thatched roofs built in front.

The caves were simple and unadorned. They had stone floors, low ceilings and white-washed walls. We had very hard beds, a few chairs, a simple desk, a washstand and, in one cave, we even had a wooden bath. The cave dwellings were poorly protected against heat in summer and cold in winter.

I often had nightmares on winter nights when the wind howled outside the cave like furious ghosts calling from another world. Father, who usually worked through the night, would lower the wick of the lamp to save on fuel, before walking over to my bedside to comfort me. Taking my hands into his, he would say, "It's only the wind, Little One! There are no ghosts or robbers. Now close your eyes and go back to sleep. Need you have fear still, when Papa is here to protect you?" I would shake my head and smile. Yes, you silly, I told myself, Papa is strong and loving! He will never allow ghosts or robbers to harm you! Though my father dispelled my fears at such times, I often had trouble falling asleep again.

Father chain-smoked his horrible Yenan cigarettes and our cave dwelling was usually filled with smoke. I disliked to smell the pungent odor of tobacco, or hear Father suck in the smoke of his cigarette with the unpleasant noise characteristic of the peasants in central China where he came from.

Worse than the howling wintry nights were the times when I had to be awakened and taken to another cave in the middle of the night. It would have been unbearable for me if Father had not put his strong arms around me and said, "It's going to be all right, Little One, as soon as we move into the other cave across the hill." Then he would gently pat my back and continue, "We have to keep moving so the Japanese won't find us. Just think the number of bombs they are wasting on us trying to bomb the right cave!"

Perhaps it was his calm ways that made me feel less frightened. Perhaps it was the warmth I felt as he cuddled me in his arms. I think it was both. Whatever it was, I was often asleep, with my head resting on his shoulder, before we even got half way to one of the four caves among which we rotated to avoid the Japanese bombers.

Another unpleasant memory of my childhood days in Yenan was the yellow dust that filled the valley between the lowest hills. It was everywhere! Everything I had at home was coated with yellow. I often had to wear a gauze mask over my face for protection. How I grew to hate that color! To this day I make it a point not to own anything yellow!

"When we first entered Shensi," Mother told me later on, "we noticed the villagers were very poor. Even the pigs seemed thin and ill-tempered. One comes on me snarling. They snap at each other's ears like dogs! But people seemed content. In one village, I saw rugged children playing and singing with bunches of wild irises!" Except for the industries started by the Red Army, the villagers were farmers.

Pao-an, once a frontier stronghold during the T'ang dynasty against the nomadic invaders of the north, was made capital of the Chinese Communist Government until December, 1936, when Yenan became the capital and remained so for the next twelve years.

Yenan was a big city. It had a large population, a university of sorts, schools, theatre, a radio station, a hospital and a newspaper plant. In its way of life, however, it was more like a backward village. Everyone wore the same crude uniforms and lived like peasants, from the top down, even Father, who was Chairman and ruler of the nineteen Soviet governments that included several million people throughout China.

One bitter winter after another, Father wore the same tattered coat over his cotton-padded suit of strong blue cotton. There was no *folie de grandeur* in him, only the non-personal megalomania of a cause-addict who was convinced of the ultimate victory of his cause.

Mother and I each had two summer suits which the government issued to us and which we alternated every week. In winter, they were replaced by

20

cotton padded suits of similar material. Mine had faded to different tones of grey blue from lengthy exposure to the sun. Mother brightened up my clothes by knitting colorful socks and sweaters for me. She also taught me to make shoes out of heavy cotton, padded in winter, with soles of home-grown hemp.

The electricity of the Yenan radio station was produced by foot pedal. The instruments in the only hospital we had were the crudest, with very little in the way of medical supplies from the outside world. Father urged chemists, biologists and physicians to experiment with local herbs, in order to replenish our store of medicine.

Food was primitive and scarce. On every little clearing, people grew their own vegetables. One very important event in my childhood was when toward sunset every late afternoon, I helped my father work in his garden where he grew his own tobacco and tomatoes. Whenever he found a plump red tomato, he would give it to me secretly. "Eat this quickly, before Mother sees you with it. She'll be angry at me for spoiling your appetite for supper."

My friends and I worked and studied long hours in cold, damp, dimly lit public buildings. Candles and kerosene were too expensive, so most of the time we used home-pressed vegetable oil in tiny jars with a hanging cotton wick. If we were lucky, sometimes we were allowed to read in public halls that were lit by big oil lamps hanging from the ceiling. These were bright, but they fluctuated. To our merriment, the burner would sometimes explode, providing diversion for us youngsters, from the rigid routine of learning.

I did not mind school at all, and did well in every subject I undertook. Most of all I loved to read and write, aptitudes inherited from my parents. When I did especially well in school, my parents would let me stay up to watch the Saturday night Dance, the chief social event of the week in Yenan.

The hall and the band were crude, but the easy fellowship among the adults turned crudities into fun. I especially enjoyed the two special duties I was assigned, sprinkling water on the floor to keep the dust down, and passing out peanuts with the order: "Throw your shucks behind your chairs and not on the dance floor!"

The dance-hall windows were always open, even in winter, since people danced in their padded clothes. Once, after I had sprinkled water on the floor, water drops began to freeze near the windows, and not being careful, I slipped on the ice, scattering my bag of peanuts all over the floor. Startled, everybody stopped dancing. Some of them pointed their fingers at me affectionately and, clucking their tongues, said, "Remember, Ch'ang-ch'eng, throw your shucks behind your chairs and not on the dance floor!" I was never more embarrassed in my whole life!

Nobody had any peanuts that night and I sat by Father and watched people dance to rhythms of such American favorites as *Old Black Joe* and *On Top of Old Smoky* played on Chinese musical instruments. There were waltzes, two-steps and four-steps. I paid special attention to Uncle Chou En-lai whenever there was a waltz, because he was perfection in it. I imagine he exercises the same control and easy grace in all of his diplomatic negotiations! Uncle Liu Shao-chi, who, next to Father, was the leading Marxist theoretician, danced with a scientific precision in which two plus two are equal to four. Uncle Chu Teh, Commander-in-chief of the armies, danced as if he were still doing his famous Long March. He kept a steady one-step, no matter what the band played.

While Mother danced with the other leaders, Father sat and talked with his comrades. When the band announced the last dance, Father hurried over to me and said jokingly, "Little One, will you do your Papa the honor ..." Before he could finish, I had jumped up from my chair and was leading him to the dance floor. Father had his own firm and delicate sense of rhythm. He never really submitted to or followed the music that was being played. As his partner, I had to pay close attention and yield watchfully and to move at slight indications. Father was not a good dancer. But it was a triumph for me to dance with him and to stay up way past my bedtime!

Toward the end of my first year in school, I won first prize in an essay contest. As a reward, I was allowed to meet one of Father's foreign visitors. At the sight of the strange-looking western "devil" with blond hair, blue eyes and big nose, I could only stand there with my mouth wide open, unable to speak.

Frozen with fright, I just stared. Then, seizing a piece of candy right out of the man's hand, I raced out, not daring to look back. Mother made me go back afterwards to apologize and thank the generous guest, who was so pleased with me that he gave me another little package which contained a can of butter. Mother bought two eggs so I could make a foreign dish with the butter. That night, with Mother's help, I made a delicious omelette for supper. For the next four evenings, my omelette was featured at our table. I don't think my parents liked butter very much, but they pretended to like my omelette. They did not want to hurt my feelings. I can imagine how happy they must have been when the little can of butter finally ran out!

Despite the lack of modern facilities, and the war with Japan, my childhood days in Yenan remain in my mind a haven of peace and happy memories.

I lived a carefree, primitive life, very close to nature and with no sense of hurry. Although I worked hard, I felt a sense of the ages, of time and space, of the earth and the slow even rhythm of the seasons. I felt close to the wide, harsh expanse of the land, and the slow spin of the sun above it, bringing seedtime and harvest.

I remember once stepping out from the cave at dawn and finding myself directly under the sky. In the vastness, I became more aware of every rain drop, every snow-flake, and every changing position of the heavenly bodies. I remember the countless summer afternoons, when my friends and I swam naked in the Yen River which divides Yenan into two and the banks of which were also yellow except for the meadows on either side which were green, and we were darker than the earth! Even in the midst of winter, when our food supply was rationed and we had to limit to two meals a day, I rejoiced in the new falls of snow that was "so good for the crops."

I will always cherish memories of those first ten years of my life when I was Father's favorite. He was already a very important man then, but he always found time to be with me. He was loving, gentle, understanding and much less strict than Mother.

Mother was gentle and loving too, but she was very firm with me. She was very quiet by temperament. She always seemed to me to be sad. She looked happy only when Father was around. Then her eyes would sparkle and there would be a smile on her lips. After Father lost interest in her, she became even less talkative than before and her rare smiles became rarer still. Sometimes she forced herself to smile out of maternal love for me, but then her eyelids and her lips would tremble. It was painful for me to watch her.

I remember vividly the day her world and mine fell apart, when Father told her that he would soon leave her.

School was let out early that afternoon and Mother had not expected me to be home. When I got to our cave, the door was ajar, so I peeped inside.

Mother was crying and Father was sitting at his desk with his back to her. "Maybe," she said, her voice soft and bitter, "you ought to keep that actress as your mistress and spare yourself some strong opposition." "It's all over with us," he said calmly.

Still sobbing, Mother said, "Nine years I have been your wife and companion. How can you have the conscience to abandon me now?"

26

I wanted to cry, but I knew I must not, for Mother would be annoyed. She always told me that I must be brave and suffer in silence. But alone at night, I wept. For days I remained inconsolable. I would go along feeling flat, empty, dull, and all of a sudden, I would dissolve in a heavy choking grief.

Mother grieved alone, too. One day, I found her sitting on her bed, staring into space. Her lips were moving as if in prayer. Sitting erectly in our shabby cave, she looked fatigued and anxious. The fluctuating light from the candle showed her face to be grim with determination. Her face was that of a sensitive person compelled by her own nature to face the world's hardness without shrinking, and to combat its cruelty without hatred. The expression of her eyes showed the suffering love had caused her. There was a lift to her chin, a distant look in her eyes as though she were more aware of her lonely destiny than her surroundings. She had the detachment of one who was conscious of seeing more in life than others.

I, too, felt the embrace of a lonely destiny, and tears welled up in my eyes. Rushing to her side, I put my little arms around her neck and comforted her. "Mama, don't be sad. Everything is going to be all right." Then for the first time, I cried convulsively on her shoulder and was not reproached for my maudlin weakness. Stroking my hair, she said,

"My poor little girl! How you must have suffered! You must not be troubled by what happened between Father and me. He's still a good father and you must not love him any less." "But Mother," I said, "it just seems strange that he can be attracted to another woman and be so heartless to leave you after what you've meant to each other." "In the heart of man, Ch'ang-ch'eng," she replied, "nothing is strange. Someday when you are a woman, you'll understand why I can forgive your father even when he ceases to love me. You see, Ch'ang-ch'eng, a man's love for a woman is only a part and not the entirety of his human existence. It is a diversion for him, something like a song. He wants at times to sing and it is a happy thing to do so. But he cannot spend his whole life in song, or to sing the same tune all the time!" I did not fully understand Mother's words, but I nodded my head anyway. I was deeply moved by my mother's true affection for my father. Warmth, for a moment, overlay my every other emotion and I felt closer to Mother than ever before.

Shortly afterwards, Mother and I left for Moscow where we remained until the winter of 1948.

Father came to say good-bye to me at the railway station. He give me a delux edition of *Monkey*, a folk novel of China, and several other books that he had read as a child. When he wanted to kiss me good-bye, I turned away. The last thing he said to

28

me before my departure was: "How fast you can forget your Papa, Little One!"

The truth is I never forgot. How I wanted him to ask Mama and me to stay on in Yenan with him. How I longed to have him cuddle me in his arms as he once did. But most of all, I wanted him to love Mama again.

Alone in the train compartment, my numbness gave way to heavy, uncontrollable sobs. As we sped toward Russia, I felt a sudden chill churning and tightening my gut. My throat went raw. And all at once I felt the chill in my stomach grow to fear—fear of uncertainty, fear of living in a strange land among strange people.

Although Mother had the opportunity to become an author writing from abroad, and I, the opportunity to learn and become proficient in several foreign languages, Mother could not be comforted. There were always unshed tears in her eyes, and a shadow of grief hung like a veil over her face, a shadow which never left her. Nowadays even in her moment of joy when she is with my two children, a mysterious sadness still mists her eyes. Her abnormally large eyes have, at times, seemed to contain all the sadness in the world.

Of the five daughters she bore as a result of nine years of cohabitation with Father, two years as his mistress and seven years as his wife, I am the only one she has now. My four older sisters were left in the care of local peasants during the Long March, and to this day we are still trying to find their whereabouts.

I have, or more precisely, did have, two older step-brothers, An-ying and Yung-fu, sons of Father's second wife, Yang K'ai-hui. An-ying was killed in 1951 during the Korean war. When An-ying was alive, Father's critics dubbed him "Prince Mao". Yung-fu is working as a minor official somewhere in China. I have two younger step-sisters also, Lina and Mao Mao, daughters of Father's present wife, his fourth.

She is Lan Ping, known today as Chiang Ching, a name Father gave her after she maneuvered her way into his cave-dwelling in Yenan. She has been a very powerful political figure since the beginning of the Cultural Revolution in 1966 which plunged China into chaos.

As time went on, she and I learned to tolerate each other. Sometimes she even stays to talk to me when I visit Father in his official residence, a one-story house in Peking where my step-sisters also live.

My visits are never publicized because in my country, the private lives of public figures are considered to be of little consequence, and they are seldom emphasized. So it is with Father, perhaps the most powerful and most adulated man in the history of China.

Mother was right. I understand now and am able to forgive and love Father without bitterness.

Although I respect him as a great leader, I repudiate his political philosophy of dictatorship by idea, in China. He advocates that daily life of the people is not and must not be any other than political life. In so doing, his brand of 'ism' would open the door to the tyranny of a corporate design.

As a writer, I advocate freedom for the creative personality. But Father, an advocate of the dictatorship by idea, distrusts any freedom of thought.

I respect the dignity of each person, and the fellowship of all persons too much to be in complete accord with him.

He insists that literature should serve the state. I maintain that good literature has to be free and spontaneous, without deliberate preparation.

It is not surprising, however, that despite the lack of freedom to think, millions in China revere and adulate him. After all, he is the one who drove out the foreigners and restored to China much of its former power and self-respect.

Not having to go through the humiliation that China did in the century following the Opium War, foreigners cannot know the corporate emotion that comes with the sudden recovery.

Father has always been a politician with the vocation of an educator!

He has transformed China from a prostrate and

humiliated nation into a strong and self-sufficient nation. The metamorphosis not only alters the balance of power in Asia, but also assumes primary importance in the strategic thinking of the world.

His teachings have transformed the Chinese people, long known to be loose as sand as a people, into a unified, well-disciplined people devoted to the building of a strong nation.

Some of his writings were put into a book entitled *Quotations from the Works of Chairman Mao.* It reportedly sold 330,000,000 copies between June 1966 and March 1967, when it was first printed. It is fast becoming a best seller of all time, second only to the Bible.

One quarter of the world's population daily quote him and sing his praises.

We hang his portrait with reverence everywhere, in our homes, in our schools and public buildings just as others would display pictures and statues of their gods.

Numerous books and articles have been written about him. Yet facts about his personal life are often just glossed over, or in some cases, never even mentioned. These facts are frequently contradictory. Rarer still are the facts about his four wives and his nine children.

Mother frequently says that I am more of a Mao

than a Ho because of my fondness for reading and my likings for aphorism.

Unfortunately, my resemblance to Father in the later is only superficial. I am full of sayings that I quote from others, while Father is full of originals that he ad libs as he converses.

On the subject of man-woman relationship he has three sayings I know about:

"The silliest woman can manage a clever man!"

"Behind every great man there is a woman."

"Marriage must be a relation either of sympathy or of conquest."

No woman, however clever, can manage Father if she does not have charm and beauty.

When he was fourteen, Grandfather married him to a peasant girl of twenty. During the elaborate wedding ceremony, when Father lifted the veil from the bride's face and saw her for the first time, he did not like what he saw. Andre Malraux, the famous French statesman once said in jest, "Mao took one look at his first woman and ran! And he has been running ever since!" There were no children because Father refused to consummate the arranged marriage.

Mother once asked Father about it and his answer was brief. "I never lived with her and I never considered her to be my wife." Mother is not one to pry, so to this day, nobody knows how long Father's first wife stayed with the family.

Grandfather was of course very upset by Father's defiance. He and father never got along because they were both very stubborn. Grandfather frequently beat and humiliated Father and my two uncles, Tse-min and Tse-tan, both of whom were killed by Father's enemies, the former in 1943, the latter in 1935.

Their father was a severe taskmaster, who forced his three sons as well as his only daughter, Tse-hung, to labor long hours in the fields. My aunt Tse-hung was also executed by Father's enemies in 1930.

Father disliked the monotonous farm chores and felt restless living at home. At the age of sixteen, he left home to strike out on his own.

Although Father hated his father when he was young, he was able to speak of him later with some objective appreciation.

Once he told Mother, "My father's discipline probably benefited me. It made me diligent; it made me keep my family's accounts carefully."

Father had long since outgrown personal hostility toward Grandfather, whom he now sees as a product of a decaying society.

I understand that the pattern of father rejection runs through the lives of many of Father's fellow revolutionists.

Behind Father, the great Chairman Mao, there were two women: his mother, and his second wife, Yang K'ai-hui.

Grandmother was a kind woman. Religious, generous and sympathetic, she was ever ready to share what she had. She was born Wen Ch'i-mei in Hsiang Hsiang, Hunan, a place not far from her husband's village of Shao Shan, Hunan. Grandmother was a dutiful wife and often acted as buffer between her ill-tempered husband and their sons. She imparted to Father, her first born, the virtues of kindness and generosity.

Yang K'ai-hui was a beautiful, brilliant woman whom Father truly loved as wife and companion.

In 1957, twenty-seven years after her death by execution, Father dedicated a poem, entitled "The Gods" to her, calling her his Proud Poplar because her surname Yang means poplar.

The Gods[1]

My proud poplar is lost to me, and to you, your
    willow.
As poplar and willow, they soar to the
    highest heaven.
They asked Wu Kang what he had given them.
He presented them wine from the cassia tree.

1. In a Chinese legend, Qu Kang, who sought immortality, the secret of which was supposed to be in the possession of the Goddess of the Moon, was condemned to cut down the cassia tree on the moon. The tree became whole again as soon as his axe had done its work.

Chang O, the lonely goddess on the moon,
    spreads her wide sleeves
to dance for these good souls in the illimitable
    sky.
Words come down on earth of the tiger's defeat.
Their tears fall like torrential rain.

(May 11, 1957)

Although Father loved Yang K'ai-hui deeply, he was vulnerable, and at the age of thirty-five, while fighting a guerilla war in Kiangsi Province, he started to live with my mother, who was seventeen years his junior. Yang had stayed behind in Hunan. After the first two years of his marriage to Yang which was the happiest and the most romantic period in Father's life, he had to endure long separations from her. However, their marriage, which lasted ten years, was described by friends and foes alike, as an ideal romance.

Mother's marriage to Father was a relation of sympathy and of conquest. They needed each other when they first met in Kiangsi. Father was lonely because his second wife, K'ai-hui, was imprisoned in Changsha by the war lord Ho Chien. Mother was young and innocent and needed to love and to be loved. He declared his love for her when she was at the threshold of womanhood and she willingly gave herself to him even though she knew he rightfully belonged to another woman.

Father was attracted to Mother's youth and unusual beauty; he was mesmerized by her quiet fortitude.

In the Chinese version of Snow's *Red Star Over China*, he wrote, in his own caligraphy, that Mother had led a women's detachment during the Nangchang Uprising in 1928, which is officially considered the beginning of the revolution.

He loved her then, and was a most devoted husband throughout the hard years of war and the seemingly endless year of the Long March.

There were tales, told to me by "Old Tree Trunks", as survivors of the March are nicknamed, that Father used to ride back to the medical corps to see Mother at the risk of his own life.

However, he lost interest in her after the Long March, when Mother was a physical wreck and appeared aged beyond her years.

He took the greatest risk in his career when in 1937 he petitioned for a divorce. Divorce was unheard of among the upper level of the Chinese Communist Party members, and to divorce one's faithful companion of the Long March could be political suicide.

Indeed he must surely have fallen under the spell

of the seductive Lan Ping, a Shanghai starlet twenty years his junior.

Lan Ping, a native of Shantung Province in Northern China, though not beautiful, was not unattractive in her youth. With her voluptuous figure, large eyes, double eyelids, fair skin and tall fine body, she attracted many young men as well as Father, who, at forty-four, greatly enjoyed the attention of a much younger woman. She was an actress, a woman of the world. In those days, the ratio of men to women was eighteen to one. She stood out, as we Chinese say, like a stork among chickens, compared to Mother and most of the other women cadres in Yenan.

Mother, in her worn Lenin-style tunics and with her coarse hands and feet, though more proletarian, was certainly less appealing. She did not grant Father the divorce until 1947. For nine years Lan Ping lived with him as his common-law wife. A great many of Father's followers, especially the students, were greatly disappointed because they had always thought Father to be an austere revolutionary puritan whose only vice was his addiction to chain smoking.

In the 1950's, world opinion of Father fell into two diametrically opposed patterns. Some regarded him as a true successor of China's great scholar-emperors, visionary revolutionaries and warrior-poets. Others regarded him as an inhuman despot murdering tens of millions in his vain attempt to force his unrealistic doctrines on reality.

As he began the third decade of his rule, the world finally accepted his government in China and his socialist revolution as the most portentous event of the century. A Communist government is firmly established in China. It is not merely an interlude of pointless mass suffering soon to be forgotten in the annals of Chinese and world history.

Today Father is the undisputed ruler of the People's Republic of China. More than any period in the history of China, the fate of the individual Chinese, the Chinese nation and East Asia as a vital sector of world politics, depended much upon his character, which, fortunately, is flexible in the face of national expediency.

He showed extreme flexibility when safe in the Shensi retreat from the Nationalists, he carried out a large-scale economic and social reorganization within the territory he controlled. By 1936, however, the invasion of Northern China by Japan spurred him on to join with the Nationalists against Japan. He offered a compromise program that included:

1. Resistance against Japan
2. Reorganization of fiscal and tax structure
3. Development of trade and industry

4. Improvement of educational facilities and the working and living conditions of the people
5. Cooperation with friendly foreign powers

These terms were rejected by Chiang K'ai-shek, who, instead, ordered Chang Hsueh-liang, a young general stationed in Manchuria, to wipe out the Communists. However, Chang did not carry out his order. While Chiang was attending a conference in Sian, he ordered the arrest of Chang Hsueh-liang. But Chang's supporters kidnapped Chiang who grudgingly agreed to join troops with the Communists against Japan. The kidnapping incident became known as the Sian Incident of 1936.

The two forces fought together until Japan surrendered in 1945. The Communists fought some of the bitterest encounters in guerrilla warfare. Peasants supported them and many Nationalists troops defected to them. When the Japanese withdrew forces under terms of the surrender, the Communists took over areas previously occupied by them. Civil war threatened to break out between the Nationalists and the Communists immediately after World War II.

Stalin counseled the Chinese Communists to dissolve their army and join in a coalition government with Chiang Kai-shek. The United States sent Ambassador P. J. Hurley to Yenan to persuade

Father to go to Chungking and meet with Chiang for the purpose of ending all fighting in China. Under the protection of the Americans, Father went to Chungking August 28, 1945. It was on this plane trip that he wrote "Snow", his best known poem.

Snow

The scene is the north lands.
A thousand leagues sealed in ice,
A myriad leagues of blowing snow.
On either side of the Long Wall,
I see only one vastness.
Up and down the Yellow River
Torrents are frozen.
Mountains are like dancing silver snakes
And hills like waxen elephants, climbing to the
    sky.
On sunny days
With added elegance one sees the red of the sun
    against a gleaming white.
Such is the beauty of the land,
Countless heroes bow their heads in tribute.
The first emperors of Ch'in and Han Dynasties
Lacked literary brilliance,
The founders of Tang and Sung
Had but few artistic grace,
And Genghis Khan

Knew only how to shoot vultures with arrows.
They are all gone now.
If we are to count men of vision,
We have to seek among the present generation.

He wrote the poem in the airplane. It was the first time he had been in an airplane. He was astonished by the beauty of China from the air.

"My poems are so stupid—" he told Robert Payne, an author, in Yenan a year later, "you mustn't take them seriously."

The truce soon collapsed and Communist troops rapidly defeated the Nationalists. City after city fell like ripe plums and the Nationalists withdrew to the island of Taiwan.

On October 1, 1949, Father proclaimed, in his quiet voice: "The Central Governing Council of the People's Government of China today assumes power in Peking."

Thousands of voices cheered from TIEN AN MEN, The Gate of Heavenly Peace, where in centuries past tribute-bearers from all over the world made their way to the throne on their knees.

After 1949, the People's Republic of China tried to rehabitate a war-torn nation where millions were starving, not by land redistribution alone, or a return to a barter economy, but by converting it into a great industrial state. Lacking trained technicians and capital, it sought assistance from the Soviet Union. In February, 1950, China signed the Soviet-Chinese Pact, a treaty of friendship, alliance, and mutual assistance.

When the Korean war broke out in June, 1950, the Peking government followed Russia in support of the North Koreans. When General MacArthur's armies reached the Yalu River on the Manchurian border, Father sent large Chinese armies into North Korea.

After the Korean war, China continued to push forward their industrialization program and voice their strong opposition to the presence of the United States Seventh Fleet patrolling the coast of Taiwan.

In an effort to expedite its industrialization and agricultural programs, the year 1958 was designated as the beginning of the Great Leap Forward. Father ordered the formation of People's Communes, in a bold effort to surge ahead of Russia in the struggle toward a completely Communistic society.

It failed miserably. And to make matters worse, the Soviets withdrew almost all technical assistance. Father's government formally broke with Kruschev's government. Father was also succeeded as Chairman of the People's Republic by Liu Shaochi, but retained top leadership as chairman of the Politburo of the Chinese Communist Party.

We did not die from the failures of the Great Leap Forward. Rather we learned and recovered from it, by our own unaided efforts. So much so, Father feared that the new generation of Chinese might be going soft and so, he felt it necessary to rejuvenate the country with continuous revolutionary fervor, by launching the Great Proletarian Cultural Revolution of 1966.

It produced instant chaos. The nation would have been thrown into complete turmoil if Premier Chou En-lai had not been able to keep effective contact with local administrations. Although Father makes important decisions and directs the operations of his party, Premier Chou is the one who attends to administrative affairs in China.

It is perhaps rather difficult for Westerners to understand Father's goal in the Cultural Revolution. This is because Father is not an ordinary person who can be judged by any western standards of rationale. He is an exceptional man, with exceptional pride and dreams. Unless you understand his dreams, pride, confidence, and ambitions, it would be most difficult to understand his motives.

To most Chinese, the Cultural Revolution is not a movement initiated by the Chairman in his old age to wrest power from his opponents as most westerners seem to imply, but a spiritual revolution that touches the human soul. It is a movement to rid the

44

minds of the ego, and replace it with public spirit. Due to human weakness, it is difficult to cleanse the minds of private desires such as the yearning for an easy life, or personal advancement, so that the individual must first rid himself of personal desires. Unless one does this, his mind will be occupied by revisionistic thoughts.

Unleashed during the Cultural Revolution, teen-age Red Guards publicly attacked all that was foreign, bourgeois, traditional or revisionist. Operations of the Communist Party in China were paralyzed during the early period of the political upheaval. However, the Chinese people are a patient and resilient people, and once again they sprang back.

By sheer hard work and diligence, China is relatively calm and prosperous as the 1970's ushered in the third decade of Communist rule. It is marked by material progress as well as political gains in the arena of international politics.

The People's Republic of China was admitted to the United Nations on October 25, 1971, by a vote of 76 to 35 and 17 abstentions. Thus, at long last, she has taken her place in the family of nations, a place that is rightfully hers but that was so long denied her.

While the feud goes on between her and the Soviet Union, China is seeking closer ties with the West, especially with the United States. Beginning May, 1973, the United States stationed a diplomatic representative in Peking who performs in the capacity of an ambassador.

How could China, a country that was war-torn, backwards and politically disunited twenty-four years ago, rise to what she is today—a land where starvation and illiteracy are practically nonexistent? Ask any common man on the street in China, and he will surely say to you: "It's because of Chairman Mao! He is our Great Helmsman! He is our savior!"

I am not a political diarist or a journalist and I don't intend to write a political biography of my father, although some of the politics will inevitably enter the story. Whenever one writes about the latter part of Father's life, one inevitably has to analyze his political career. Since becoming Chairman of the Chinese Communist Party at the Tsunyi Conference of the Politburo in 1935, he has become so much part of his mission that it is impossible to separate his public and private lives. As his image grew from the man-of-the-people to superhuman legendary size, it has also become difficult to separate myth from fact concerning his life.

Primarily, Father fascinates me as a man, not as the great Chairman Mao, who had become a sort of demigod in the eyes of my countrymen.

He is seventy-nine years old at this writing and is

in good health. He seldom appears in public and often enjoys the solitude of his private study where books litter every shelf, table and chair.

A few months ago, my step-sister Mao Mao gave me a picture of Father's meeting with President Nixon. I keep it in my scrapbook. I have three other pictures of my father in my scrapbook. One was taken in 1949, when he entered the Capital of Peking after the Red Army defeated the Nationalists who retreated to the island of Taiwan. In it Father wears a well-pressed jacket of good woolen fabric and his face is plump and glowing. His hair is covered by a spotless sun-helmet. He looks proud and victorious.

The second shows him standing behind a long banquet table among Russian leaders during his visit to Moscow in December, 1949. In this picture he wears the stern dignity of a brooding god surrounded by lesser gods. Stalin, with his exaggerated mustache and his amiable air of self-assertion, is unimpressive beside Father.

The third photo shows him standing among other Chinese leaders. Father, a head taller than the tallest of them, stands straight and stiff. His face is set, rigid, and has an expression of his sense of mission. He has the air of a man who is not only self-confident but is completely aware that he is the Great Man.

The fourth is the one taken with the Americans, that my step-sister gave me. He is sitting in his private study, flanked by Premier Chou En-lai, President Nixon and President Nixon's advisor, Henry Kissinger. Father seems relaxed, his trousers and tunic slightly crumpled. His face, though showing signs of old age, has a relaxed, benign expression. His smile is grandfatherly. This is my favorite picture of him, because he looks so content and at peace with himself.

In the twilight of his life, Father seems to turn more and more to Confucian philosophy for introspection. His latest advice to us about grain storage comes from an ancient quote that was given to the last Emperor of the Ming dynasty which ruled China from 1368 to 1644.

"Dig tunnel deep, store grain everywhere, never seek hegemony."

While he spends most of his waking hours in the privacy of his studies, somewhere in China his subjects are either quoting his *Selected Works* or singing:

> "In the Mao Tse-tung era, the Chinese people are happy,
> the land is beautiful.
> The East is red from the rising sun,
> In China appears Mao Tse-tung,

He works for the people's welfare,
He is the people's great savior.

Chairman Mao loves the people,
He is our guide.
He leads us onward
To build a new China.

Beloved Chairman Mao,
Sun in our hearts!
Your light shines for us
In whatever we do.
We feel you nearby
Wherever we go.

He lives in splendid seclusion, and school children everywhere in China are singing, as an enormous flag with five yellow stars superimposed on a red field flutters in the wind.

Arise, you who refuse to be slaves
Our very flesh and blood will build a new Great
Wall
A savage indignation fills us now,
Arise, arise, arise!

The national anthem of the People's Republic of China proclaimed in 1949, is the same song that was sung by the Communist troops for nearly two decades before Father and his comrades came to power.

"Mao Chu Hsi wan sui!" "May Chairman Mao live ten thousand years!" Eight hundred million Chinese, a quarter of the human race, cheer.

Children at play sing:

Mao Tse-tung is like the sun
He is brighter than the sun
Little brother, little sister
Everyone clap hands
Come and sing!

With all the tenacity and stubbornness of a fiery Hunanese peasant, Father has chartered his course and followed it to his eightieth year. Can any man do more?

No matter what the outcome, history will not only name him as the unifier and defender of the Chinese people against any foreign encroachment, it will list him among the great leaders of the world.

Well then, who is this man who dared to upset the twenty-five-century old traditional way of life and thought? Was his childhood and youth different from that of ordinary men?

Let's go back to the very beginning.

1.

Birth of a Son

"One lamp is better than three candles."
Chinese proverb

"There are three things which are unfilial, and to have no posterity is the worst of them all."
Mencius

BIRTH OF A SON

On December 26, 1893, in the village of Shao
Shan, Hunan, a province in central China, Mao Jen-
sheng, my grandfather, was pacing nervously outside his house.

The moon was bright and the wintry wind was
blowing gently. "Ah! It's a good night for the
coming of my son! Now my venerable Father will
have a grandson to warm his old bones!" he muttered. "But why doesn't that useless old woman let
me in so I can see my child? She has had plenty of
time to cleanse the New Born!" He pounded his fist
against the palm of his hand and cursed the midwife
under his breath.

Tsou Ma, the village mid-wife, was the next-door
neighbor whose family shared the simple house in
the high walled courtyard with the Mao family. She
was wakened from her sleep around midnight when
Mao Jen-sheng, dispensing with polite forms,
pounded frantically at her door. "Tsou Ma, come
quick! My woman's time has come!"

"Calm down, Jen-sheng," she said to the nervous
Mao. "The way you shake all over, folks would

think you're going to have the baby instead of your wife."

Tsou Ma had never liked her neighbor. She thought he was ill-tempered, money-grabbing, and too domineering.

She avoided having anything to do with him because he always went around with a cold, hard expression on his face. He wore a goatee, his nose was rather long, and his eyebrows a trifle too bushy.

"Actually, Ch'i-mei is not due for another week or so, but I suppose all that hard work she does in the field hastened her time," she said in a harsh, sarcastic tone, as if to reproach Mao for his thoughtlessness toward his wife.

Mao Jen-sheng was a typical Hunan peasant. He had a fiery temper and a passion for land. Unlike some of his meeker neighbors, who barely existed by tilling lands that were often not their own, he was aggressive and would stop at nothing in his grim determination to better the status of his family.

"Why do babies pick such early hours to be born!" the old woman grumbled.

But that was three hours ago, and now Mao Jen-sheng was getting impatient because Tsou Ma had poked out her head only once to tell him that it was a baby boy. It bothered Mao greatly not to know if his baby son was big and healthy.

Suddenly he stopped pacing and yanked off one

cluster of red peppers growing by the lily pond just outside the courtyard. Popping one into his mouth, he chewed it noisily.

Natives of Hunan are known throughout China for their addiction to hot peppers and their fiery dispositions. In addition to the abundant small red peppers that can be seen clustered in every free space, Hunan also produces two other crops in abundance: rice and revolutionaries. There is a saying here that China can be conquered only when all the people of Hunan are dead!

Having finished his red pepper, Mao Jen-sheng was about to pop another one into his mouth when Tsou Ma called loudly to him. "You can come now! Never in my midwife life have I seen such a big, strong baby. He gave us a hard time!" The old woman's sharp voice echoed in the stillness of dawn.

The baby was crying and kicking when Tsou Ma put him into swaddling clothes.

According to the custom then, Mao Jeng-sheng paid Tsou Ma one whole dollar. Had the baby been a girl, the fee would only have been half-a-dollar.

Despite fatigue, the new mother looked beautiful. Her eyes sparkled, expressing her happiness and contentment. Her husband's unusual gentleness toward her had fostered the blossoming of maternal beauty.

55

"You are a good wife, Ch'i-mei!" Mao Jen-sheng said. "You've given me a son! Now my filial duty is fulfilled. My venerable Father is well pleased and said for you to rest in bed, and for me to cook ginger in red wine and brown sugar for you, so you'll be properly nourished."

As Mao coaxed his wife to eat up the ginger he had cooked in red wine and brown sugar, his hard face softened, and he thought of the future. Yes, I need more sons like this one, big and strong, to till my fields.

He beamed with satisfaction as he looked out the window and saw the rich dark furrowed earth surrounding the family dwelling. He had just bought back his small farm which he inherited but had lost five years ago, when he fell into debt after returning home from the army as a foot soldier. Even after paying all his debts, his girdle was laden with silver dollars, almost enough to buy the acre of land adjacent to the family farm. He was so happy at this moment he did not mind Tsou Ma's idiot son's shrilling voice chanting the doleful but popular village song:

"Over the heads of every peasant are three
swords: debts, taxes and high interest.
And before the eyes of every peasant are
three roads: to run away, to be killed, or to be
jailed."

Turning to his wife, he said, "That idiot is at it again! But the song doesn't apply to us anymore! You'll see, in another year or so, I'll have additional land and a business!" He paused, grinned and then added, "But Good Woman, you'll have to give me more sons. I can't manage any business without sons to work the fields."

Their first born, whom they named Tse-tung, flourished on the young mother's abundant milk.

The proud father was disappointed the following year when his wife did not give birth to another child, but felt compensated a year later, when another son arrived. They named their second son Tse-min. He was not as big nor as strong as Tse-tung. And as if to make amends, within the next eight years, Heaven blessed the Mao household with another stalwart son, Tse-tan, and a daughter whom Mao Jen-sheng reluctantly named Tse-hung.

"Aiya! I was hoping for another son! But we got a female slave instead!" he complained.

2

Helper in the Field

"Never attempt to catch two frogs with one hand."
                                        Chinese Proverb

HELPER IN THE FIELD

Tse-tung had to forget that he was just a little boy as he helped his mother around the house caring for his little brothers and sister. When he was but eight years old, his father put him to work in the fields.

At first he had to sit on a wicker platform in the fields and screech to frighten the birds away when rice seeds were planted. After the first few minutes of screeching, young Mao's voice became hoarse and so he stopped to rest. When his father found him sitting there idle, he screamed, "Screech, you lazy son of a turtle egg! Don't just sit there like a scarecrow! The birds will eat up all the rice seeds."

And so the young Mao kept on screeching while the hot sun beat down on his bare back. Even though he only wore a pair of blue cotton pants, he felt miserable in the heat. All the while he felt his father's eyes on him, viewing his lanky figure with distaste.

Secretly he alternated his screechings with brief moments of boyish romantic day-dreaming. He looked forward to the time when school would be in session. He was not particularly fond of learning the

Confucian classics in school, but was glad to escape the attention of his stern father who controlled all his waking hours at home.

At the village school, the eight-year-old Mao learned the Chinese characters and *li*. *Li* was roughly translated as "propriety", but it meant more. It was the sum total of moral rules, of the canons of proper conduct. It was a guide to approved behavior in all the details of daily life.

Young Mao filed into the classroom with his friends. They sat on bamboo stools, like statues, not daring to move, and received instructions from the teacher in the Chinese classics. They learned by rote, repeating the lines over and over at the top of their lungs, until the teacher was convinced that the lesson had been imprinted on their memory.

Disloyalty to the ruler is want of filial piety.

Not having self-respect is want of filial piety.

Insincerity to friends is want of filial piety.

Cowardice in battle is want of filial piety.

Although young Mao shouted those lines until he knew them by heart, he secretly debated their merits. Unthinking, he sang the passages of the Confucian *Analects*, parrot-like. His body swayed in rhythm. His lips moved in reflex action, but his heart was elsewhere. With eyes closed, he dreamed of heroes and rebels of the past, who dared challenge the authority of emperors and kings.

The teacher lectured: "There are three grades of filial piety. The highest is for you to honor your parents by achievement. The lesser is for you not to disgrace yourself, thereby casting reflections on your father and your ancestors. And the least is to be able to support your parents."

"All empty words, quite meaningless for me," young Mao thought. And his teacher's sermon quickly went in one ear and out the other.

He waited impatiently for this class of Confucian *Analects* and the Four Classics to end.

His teacher, who was a severe disciplinarian, repeated a proverb before he dismissed the class: "We must do everything as our ancestors did."

This proverb in particular disturbed and angered the rebellious young Mao.

He was not happy in his present condition and he wanted a change. He grew to hate Confucianism and thought it a hindrance to his own personal happiness. According to Confucius, all virtues have their origin in *li*. And in every detail, *li* urges everyone to be obedient to his parents. Mao was not at all convinced that one should be so blindly obedient to one's parents!

Recess time at school was a happy time for him.

63

He could forget about filial duties and he could hold long discussions with his schoolmates about the present and the future. Better still, he could read fascinating stories about the overthrow of emperors and dynasties after they had exhausted their mandates from heaven.

"Why do we still think China is the center of the world when foreign barbarians are able to invade our shores and demand our Emperor to grant them special privileges and rights? Is it not time for new ways?" Mao asked his schoolmates.

His schoolmates agreed with him that the old Chinese traditions were in an advanced stage of decay. In order to save China, they suggested, change and reform are necessary.

Mao went even further, to say that rebellion was the best solution during a time of troubles. And those were troublesome times indeed. China was humiliated by foreign powers and had to grant special privileges and rights to the British, the Russians, the Germans, the French and the Japanese.

In 1894, China declared war against Japan, over the domination of Korea. China was defeated and had to sign the treaty of Shimonoseki, April 18, 1895, which called for China's cession of Formosa, the Pescadores Islands and the Liaotung Peninsula. In addition, China was to open several ports to

Japan and pay a large idemnity. Russia, France, and Germany intervened. As a result of their "benevolent" intervention, they advanced their own interests in China.

Kiaochow was leased to the Germans, Port Arthur to the Russians, Kwangchow as a base, to the French. Seeing that the other countries were receiving concessions, Britain felt she must maintain her prestige, and so Kowloon was leased to the British. Not wanting to be left out from the China trade, United States, though avoiding pursuit of exclusive privileges, insisted upon the continuation of her most-favored nation policy.

Students and intellectuals everywhere were agitating for change. Reform and rebellion were in the air.

China's land loss in 1896-1898 gave impetus for reform. In Peking, the empress dowager Tz'u Hsi, who had controlled China's affairs since 1860, continued to follow the advice of Jung Lu and Yuan Shih-kai who advocated maintenance of the status quo. Impatient with Tz'u Hsi's inaction, Sun Yat-sen led a short-lived rebellion in Canton, in 1895. Shortly after, Sun went abroad to organize revolutionary groups among the overseas Chinese. Other important reform leaders who followed more peaceful methods were K'ang Yu-wei and Liang Ch'i-ch'ao, both of whom were greatly admired by Mao when Mao was in his early teens.

K'ang Yu-wei, adviser to the emperor, decreed sweeping reforms, collectively called the Hundred Days Reform. Unfortunately, these governmental and educational reforms failed, and foreign powers continued to demand more concessions. The reformers, eager to implement their programs, plotted to eliminate the empress dowager and Jung Lu. The plot backfired and Tz'u Hsi returned to power. She imprisoned the emperor, and K'ang Yu-wei and Liang Ch'i-ch'ao barely escaped execution.

By the time Mao Tse-tung was ten years old, his father owned 3.7 acres of land and a thriving business in grain transport. In a land of beggars, his father was considered a wealthy man. But he was strict with his sons, especially his eldest son, whom he considered rebellious and every bit as stubborn as his own father, my great grandfather. Tse-tung suffered many beatings at the hands of his tyrannical father and was happy and relieved whenever his father had to go to the city to make business deals.

On one chilly November morning, Tse-tung was awakened by the sound of the gong at a nearby temple. He stretched and yawned. Curling up his long legs, he lay shivering under the cotton quilt, defenseless against the cutting morning air. Just as he was about to doze off, he was awakened by the family rooster singing, "Cock-a-doodle-doo!"

The young Mao got dressed quickly for he had much to do before school. He groped in the dark,

66

trying hard not to bump into things. He did not want
to wake up his younger brothers, his younger sister
and his mother, who were asleep in the next room.

Winter came earlier this year to Shao Shan, a tiny
village in central China where the Mao family lived
among a hundred or so other families. More than
half of them had the surname Mao! Before he went
out to the family courtyard, young Mao reached for
his scarf and cap that his mother had put on her bed
to keep warm. She sat up and whispered, *"Didi,*
maybe I should help you!"

"I'll be fine. Papa told me what to do before he
left. And don't call me *Didi* Mama! That's for little
kids. I am ten, and I am just as tall and strong as
Papa!" He would like to have added: "I can see
people calling eight year-old Tse-min *Didi* for *he*
only comes up to my waist. And a useless weakling
who can't help with anything!" Instead, he bit his
lips and remained silent.

He thought his mother fussed over Tse-min too
much. Once he had overheard her say to his father,
"Aiya! Tse-min is so weak. But how can he be
otherwise if you only give him eggs to eat! He needs
to eat meat to be strong!"

How about me! Tse-tung thought indignantly, I
am given neither meat nor egg!

His mother repeated the list of things he had to do.
"Collect the eggs. Feed the chickens and the pigs.
Then clean the chicken house and the pigsty."

This morning, the wind blew fiercely across Shao Shan's unpaved streets, raising clouds of yellow dust. Gusty wind struck young Mao's face like sharp pins.

"Aiya! Devil-wind! Why today of all days, when I have to do everything by myself!" he muttered.

While collecting the eggs, he stumbled on the family dog, who started to bark furiously. The barking made him so nervous that he dropped the water bucket on top of the chicken house. The chickens cackled and flew into the pigsty. Soon the cackling and barking developed into a discord so earsplitting that the pigs stopped eating. They started to run and grunt, "Oink, oink, oink!" In the confusion, the dog got into the pigsty. Soon Mao Tse-tung was chasing after the dog, who ran after the chickens, who fluttered after the pigs, who ran after the dog! Round and round they went. Suddenly Tse-tung stopped and leaned against the wall momentarily. He was dizzy from all that going around. Arms akimbo, he gave out a big sigh. Just then Tse-min appeared.

He was a small boy with short arms and legs. He did not smile but there was a twinkle in his almond-shaped eyes. Calmly he wooed the dog away with a bone. Then he called and talked to the chickens ever so gently, "Cluck, cluck, cluck! Follow me!" He led the chickens back to the chicken house. When the dog and the chickens were out of the pigsty, the pigs resumed their eating. All was quiet again in the courtyard. Even the wind had stopped blowing.

Tse-min stayed to help Number One Brother Tse-tung. They finished all the chores just as the sun slipped through silvery clouds and began to shine brightly.

A few minutes later, the two brothers were sitting at the table and their mother filled their bowls with steaming rice porridge and pickled vegetables. She was proud of her two older sons.

"My good children, you may each have an egg today for a job well done!" she said with a smile.

Tse-tung was so filled with good feelings that he had to share some of it with Tse-min.

"You and I make a good team, Tse-min! Today I'll let you read one of my books."

After breakfast, the two brothers ran happily to school together.

Mao Tse-tung's spirit was dampened when upon arriving at school he had to take an exam on still-life drawing, a required subject he disliked intensely. Thinking it a waste of time to have to draw not one but two pictures for the exam, he hastily put down a straight line with a semicircle over it. He called it "Half-sun, half-stone". Then on another sheet of paper, he draw an oval and entitled it "Egg".

He was the first to hand in his drawings. Clutching the books *Three Kingdoms* and *All Men are Brothers* under his arm, he left hastily, looking

69

neither to the right nor to the left. He had wanted to finish reading these books which were romanticized accounts of wars, so he could start on some other epics that were also rich in details of strategy and tactics.

His current favorite was *All Men are Brothers*. He had read it several times and each time with the same delight. He never seemed to tire of reading about its heroes who fought against the mighty to help the mass of poor peasants.

Mao took special notes on how the heroes organized the oppressed peasants into guerilla-like bands. And he admired their fearless attack on the landlords who had much superior arms. Like the heroes in *All Men are Brothers,* young Mao advocated the sharing of spoils among the poor.

The strategy of these rebels in books left an indelible mark on his young mind and greatly influenced his strategy and tactics later on when he rebelled against and fought the Nationalist government.

He stayed up all that night reading and staggered sleepily into his art class the next morning. He was reading an article by Sun Yat-sen published in *The People's Strength* when the art teacher walked past his desk.

The teacher turned to Mao and said angrily, "How dare you read when you are supposed to be drawing!" Then he took out the whip and flogged the young Mao mercilessly.

"Now let me see how funny you think your picture "Half-sun, half-stone" is! And oh yes! You are so very clever to entitle your other picture "Egg" because that's exactly what you'll be getting for a grade in this class! Egg, egg, egg!" The teacher muttered, as the whip fell on the tender rump of the defiant child. Mao bit his lips and gritted his teeth, too proud to cry out.

He ran away from school but was afraid to return home for fear of another beating from his father. He wandered toward the city.

As the afternoon shadows lengthened, he became frightened and hungry. Night came. The heavens opened up in a wild burst of rain, as if the clouds had poured themselves out in a passion of crying. The young Mao took shelter under a tree. He was dripping wet and his tears, mixed with raindrops, ran down his cheeks.

Trees made ghostly shadows all around him. The branches on them seemed to screech as they rubbed against each other in the nocturnal breeze. The barkings of dogs sounded like the howling of wolves. The croaking of frogs was like the pounding steps made by monsters and werewolves in the night. Even his own breathing sounded strange in the eerie stillness.

71

His heart pounded fiercely as if it would leap out of his rib cage when a barn owl screeched overhead. The darkness and the strange sounds of nocturnal animals made the night seem like an eternity for the hungry little boy.

After a meager breakfast of wild berries the next morning, young Mao decided to go home. He reasoned to himself: "I have a much better chance of surviving Papa's beating than a wolf's hungry bites!"

Much to his surprise, his father did not punish him and the teacher was less severe from then on. Fortunately, his excellent grades in social studies were able to balance his poor grades in art and the physical sciences.

The rest of the school year passed peacefully. Soon it was summer.

For Mao Tse-tung, the first day of summer vacation had always seemed strange because he and Tse-min were allowed to stay in bed an extra thirty minutes.

This morning, his mother had not come to wake them until six—a whole hour later than usual!

Breakfast was different too. Instead of just porridge and pickled vegetables, they had roasted peanuts and scrambled eggs.

While the children enjoyed their "luxurious" breakfast in silence, their mother said gently, "Papa has been called away on business." Then looking directly at her oldest son she continued, "Since you and Tse-min worked so hard and so well together all through the year, I thought you might like to go someplace by yourselves today."

The two brothers decided to go on a picnic and to visit a farm where silkworms were raised.

The countryside was green and fresh with trees, grass and growing crops. Everywhere they went, they saw water buffaloes, cows, and donkeys pulling plows, or helping farmers do heavy work in the fields. In the lowlands, and in terraced fields on the lower hillsides, they saw stretches of growing rice fields.

"Look over there, Tse-min!" Tse-tung said, pointing to the farmers who were flooding a nearby field, "they are making sure there's enough moisture for the growing rice plants."

They were so excited they even forgot it was lunch time until their stomachs growled noisily. "We'd better find a place to have our picnic!" They found a shady spot under a big tree on a high hillside.

Up here only tea bushes and fruit trees were growing, because it would be difficult to bring enough water to grow rice. The abundant leaves on the tree shielded them from the blazing sun.

The two brothers rested after lunch. They played shooting marbles and kicking shuttlecocks until a gentle breeze from the north blew across the hill-sides.

"Now it's cool and we must be on our way to the farm!" Tse-tung hurried his younger brother.

At the farm they saw tables and tables of silk-worms, spinning their cocoons. They looked at the gluelike fluid coming from a hole in the lower lip of each worm with wonder! The fluid hardened into silk thread when it touched the air. The worm waved its head back and forth to wind the thread around itself, forming a cocoon.

Before the farmer soaked the silk cocoons in hot water to unwind the thread, he gave the two brothers each a cocoon to keep.

"Put them in a safe place at home, and in a short time, they will turn into butterflies and lay eggs for you," the farmer said most kindly, patting the boys on their shoulders.

Though tired from the day-long outing, Tse-tung stayed up past midnight to read.

The next morning, when the sun was just peeping through pink clouds in the eastern horizon, young Mao again set out to work in the fields.

The countryside was already bustling with activity. He waved to the farmers pushing wooden carts of vegetables and fruits on their way to the market. The air was fragrant with blossoms. Mao enjoyed the morning air and thought happily: "I am going to set it free when my cocoon turns into a butterfly!"

3

A Business Transaction

"In the little boy one sees the final man."
                                    Chinese proverb

*"In serving his parents a son may plead with them;
when they do not acquiesce, he should not give up
but should show increased reverence; should the
parents punish him, he ought not murmur."*
                                    Analects.

*"Between father and son rebuke is the greatest of-
fence against that tenderness which should sub-
sist."*   *Mencius*

A BUSINESS TRANSACTION

Tse-tung left his childhood behind, in the year that followed. He did not consciously bid it farewell, but rather grew out of it, bursting into a tall, massive boy of thirteen, somewhat awkward in his speech and movements.

New longings came into his life, new concepts, new ambitions. He was bored by the monotony of doing the same farm chores day after day, week after week. He still spent long hours in solitary study, after each tiring day tilling the fields for his father.

His father was devoting more time to his thriving grain business and spent less and less time on the farm. He also delegated more responsibilities to his sons. One morning he sent Tse-tung out for an errand.

"Tse-tung, you must go and get the two hogs I bought from Farmer Liu who lives in the next village. The prices of hogs have doubled this week but I was lucky enough to have made the deals with Farmer Liu last week before the prices went up!"

His father reached into his pocket and took out two shining coins. "Here are two silver dollars for the two hogs. And don't let him talk you into paying the new prices now. Do you hear?" Mao Jen-sheng reminded his son, whom he considered somewhat of a blockhead as far as business matters were concerned.

His mother was excited and nervous for him because this was the first trip he ever took outside his home village of Shao Shan. She packed him a lunch and said before he left, "Take along this new jacket, Tse-tung. It might be cold on your way back tonight."

On the way to Farmer Liu's house, the young Mao saw a beggar lying on the roadside. The beggar was sick and had alternate attacks of chill and fever.

Young Mao stopped and tried to help. But he had no medicine to give to the sick man. Shivering, the old man groaned, "Have mercy! Young man, I am dying from cold. Blanket please!" *"Lao chia*[1], I have no blanket with me but—" Taking off his new jacket, he said, "Here, you can have my jacket." He covered the sick beggar with his new jacket, and with a heavy heart, continued on his journey.

When Mao Tse-tung arrived, Farmer Liu and his family were having their lunch. Farmer Liu offered to share their rice gruel, and salted vegetables.

[1]Literally means old family which was a common form of address to a stranger. This form of address is no longer used in China. It has been replaced by *T 'ung chih,* a term meaning comrade.

"I'm sorry that I can offer you only watery gruel. But if you can stay for supper, we'll have a thicker gruel with more rice grains in it," Liu apologized.

Though the Lius worked very hard and their diet was meager, they were generous and happy people. They held no grudge against anyone, except their tyrannical landlord. Mao felt at home with them and began to talk to them as if they were old friends.

"The landlord squeezes every possible grain out of us," Farmer Liu lamented. "If we can't pay rent, they whip us or take our daughters away as slaves to use at their pleasure."

Mrs. Liu joined in the conversation. "Everyone of us in this little village tills lands for the same landlord who lives just beyond the next hill. He is safely fenced in and protected by his henchmen! But no more of these sad tales. The whole country is full of them. Let's talk about happier things," said Farmer Liu, trying to change the subject.

"How can we talk of happier things?" Farmer Liu's wife retorted, "When we have to sell our female slave tomorrow! She is only ten, Master Mao, and she is our youngest daughter. We've already sold two others. But our yield this year is not enough to pay our rent. What's a mother to do?" Sobbing, she drew her daughter close to her and mother and daughter cried helplessly on each other's shoulders.

Young Mao was at a loss as to what he should do.

He shifted his legs and wrung his hands. The two silver dollars made a tinkling sound as he wiggled in his seat.

"I could pay them two silver dollars for just one hog," he thought. "Then they could sell the other hog for two additional silver dollars. With four silver dollars they might not have to sell their daughter. I would not hesitate to pay Farmer Liu the new price if Papa had not specifically reminded me about his lucky deals."

Young Mao thought and squirmed with indecision. "What's worse is that I've also given away my new jacket."

He could almost hear what his father would say when he came home without the jacket and minus one hog.

"You wretched one! You and your mother are two chips from the same block—always so generous with my money. How dare you disobey my specific instructions! May you be struck by lightning for your unfilial ways!"

His mother would almost certainly try to calm his father by reminding him that Buddha would be pleased by their son's generosity. "Besides," she would add, "We have plenty, Venerable husband, and others around us have so little. It's our obligation to help them!"

"A violent family war would most likely to errupt

if I don't go home with two hogs," Mao Tse-tung thought glumly.

Mrs. Liu apologized in between sobs, "I am sorry for such a show of emotion, Master Mao," and she tried hard to smile. Her tenderness touched the young Mao. It reminded him of his own gentle mother and without another moment's hesitation, he said, "Here are the two silver dollars for one hog. The prices have gone up this week. And you can still sell the other one for another two silver dollars."

Farmer Liu was grateful and he thanked Mao, "May you be blessed a thousand times, Master Mao, for your generosity! We are forever in your debt."

In the dim evening glow, Mao saw how old and wrinkled his host was. And he was only in his early thirties! His face was weather-worn to a leathery brown; his darting eyes sunken from worries and hunger; his facial muscles twitched from nervousness and insecurity. Yet underneath this seeming resignation to hopelessness, he detected a spirit in Farmer Liu, a fierce desire to better himself, that if once kindled, and if united with others in the same position as he, could sweep through the country like forest fires.

"There must be millions of Farmer Lius in China," Mao thought. "Just think what might and power they would have if they united against their common enemies the landlord, and the government

81

that pandered to the greed of the rich. In rebelling against their overlords, they would lose nothing because they had nothing to lose."

The thought of rebellion and perhaps one day of becoming a leader among these poor simple peasants, so excited young Mao that he momentarily forgot his fear of facing his irate father when he arrived home without his jacket, and just one hog.

As young Mao expected, his father almost jumped through the roof when he got home.

"You imbecile! How dare you come back with only one hog! And who gives you permission to give away your new jacket? Well, you are not going to get another jacket for the next ten winters."

His father then showered curses and Confucian quotations on him about his unfilial conduct. He answered his father with other classical quotations urging his father to be kind and affectionate toward his children. Mao Jen-sheng was furious, but he was so impressed by his son's fluency in the classics that without another word, he stormed out of the house.

Young Mao was dumbfounded. He was sure that his father was going to beat him for his defiance. For the first time in his learning years, he was glad that he had taken the trouble to memorize his classics.

"From now on," he thought, "I must equip myself with appropriate quotations to avoid further beatings."

Two weeks after the hog incident, young Mao again offended his father.

After carrying ten basket-loads of manure to the fields before sunrise, he immediately sat down in the shade and started to read.

"Ten thousand demons curse you! Why do you keep on tormenting me with your unfilial ways! Is there to be no end to spending with you? You not only waste money on those useless novels, you have to waste time reading them!" Without giving his son a chance to reply, Mao Jen-sheng slapped his oldest son mercilessly.

"Don't you dare hit me again! You unreasonable old fool!" Angrily, Mao Tse-tung ran away. "I'm never coming back!"

His mother shuddered at such display of hot temper, and knew her son was capable of violence if provoked.

She was relieved when he came back, after a week of wandering.

He was different from her other sons who were outwardly more affectionate, yet it was easy for her to love him. He was wise and compassionate.

"Your oldest one is such a learned boy!" everyone told her.

In his room there was a shelf full of books. She often caught him reading past midnight. "You must put a cloth over the window so your father will not

see the light," she said to him one night. He was so
pleased with her suggestion that he gave her a big
hug that almost knocked her off her feet!

That was the only time she saw him so light-
hearted. She sensed that he was not at peace with
himself. He was restless. Something was bothering
him. Something outside the family. Something outside the fields. Something so beyond her she
doubted she would ever understand. She caught a
few words here and there, when her sons were
talking together. *"Ke ming!* Revolution!" *"Hsin
chung kuo!* New China!" Those words meant
nothing to her except that people were killed for
uttering them.

On the way home from the fields one day, she saw
troops marching through the village.

"Those soldiers are going to Changsha, the provincial capital, to put down a rebellion there," her
Number One son told her. His face was red with
anger, his unruly jet black hair falling over his
broad, high forehead. "Soon, headless corpses will
be hung on high poles for all to see and to take heed.
Aiya! They'll destroy us all. We must have a new
government!" he muttered. She feared for her first
born.

Spring came, bringing with it torrents of rain,
lashing the fields with sudden fury, washing away
winter's dead remains, and then subsiding into

bursts of sunshine. In the clear sharp light, the countryside was breathtaking. Trees everywhere were either blooming or rich with new buds. Multicolor flowers, exuding a fresh fragrance, swayed in the gentle breeze, like changing mosaics strewn in a sea of lush green.

For the Mao family, from the very young to the very old, it was a time of furious activities. They seeded and planted. So days blended into nights, and nights into days. And soon summer was upon them.

From early morning until dusk, they watered and nurtured what they had planted. When night came, it was too hot for them to enjoy the lilacs in the courtyards. They were too weary to see the blazing summer flowers adorning the hills beyond.

Then came autumn, a time of back-breaking work, but a time of great rejoicing, for now they would reap the fruits of their labor.

"The yield has been good," his father said, breathlessly. "Eighty-four tan[1] of rice this year! It's time for celebration!" So a big feast was prepared and friends and relatives were invited.

Mother and daughter cleaned and prepared food all that day. Tables were set for the men guests who had much to eat and much to drink. *"K'ang p'ei!*

---

[1] 1 tan equals 133 ⅓ lbs.

Bottom up!" The men played a little game with the fingers before drinking and the loser had to empty his glass. There were much laughing and carousing.

The women folk served the men, and listened submissively. Later on, when the men had finished, they ate the left-overs in the kitchen, standing up like servants. Suddenly everyone was silent. The father's angry voice was heard.

"Lao t'ien! Oh heavens! What have I done to deserve an eldest son so impudent and lazy!"

"Ten thousand demons curse you, foolish Old One!" Mao Tse-tung, cursing and shouting, came to the edge of a pond in front of the house. His mother ran after him. "Please come back, my son! Don't jump, I beg of you!" "No, not until Papa promises not to beat me anymore."

Demands and counter-demands were issued for cessation of the fight between father and son.

"You are to apologize and kowtow to me as a sign of submission."

"Only a one-knee kowtow. No more!" the son retorted. The father hesitated but said presently, "Let it be done." And it was thus that the family war ended.

Triumphantly, Tse-tung said to his mother, intending for the family to hear, "Let this be a lesson for us. If we defend our rights by open rebellion,

Papa will relent, but if we remain weak and submissive, he only curses and beats us all the more. We must form a 'united front' against him!"

4

Betrothal

"Among ten matchmakers, only nine will lie."
Chinese proverb

BETROTHAL

The gong had never bothered Mao Tse-tung before. But this morning it seemed to shrill, piercing through the predawn stillness. His heart echoed with bumpity-booms. His heavy lids responded with twitches. He knew he should try to rest a while longer, lest he be unable to perform the various morning duties for his mother before setting out to the fields. But he sat up in bed and rested his chin against his knobby knees. Last night he had overheard his parents talking in the next room about his betrothal, and he had spent the whole night tossing and turning, unable to sleep. He had put his ears to the wall so he could hear every word.

"Our son is only fourteen this year. He is too young to be married. He's just a boy!" his mother said.

"Not if people see how big and tall he is. I am sure he measures over six feet now!" His father paused and then continued, "I've seen her. She's twenty and she is big and strong. She'll be worth at least one hired hand. Her father and I already cast the horoscopes of the young couple and found them well suited."

91

Tse-tung wished his brother Tse-min had not come to his room then, because he wanted to know more about this peasant girl who would soon be coming to live with him as his wife.

"Tse-tung!" His father called from the next room, "Time for you to be up! Must I waste my breath calling you every morning?"

He couldn't bear having his father heap more insults on him so he stood up. Half leaning on the side of his bed, he started to dress. The sleeves of his cotton tunic barely covered his elbows, exposing a good part of his arms with their dark purple veins. His blue trousers were too short to cover his ankles.

He splashed cold water on his face. Then he looked in the mirror to comb his hair. His eyes, which he inherited from his mother, were wide and penetrating. He smiled contentedly and quickly combed and braided his jet black hair into a queue.

"Be quick! Get going! You are crawling like an ant! Must it take you all morning to draw water from the well!"

Young Mao ignored his father's carping. He knew today his father, like everyone else in the house, was anxious to get him out to the fields. He was not to be home when the betrothal ceremony took place. He had seen enough betrothal ceremonies in the neighborhood to know exactly what would be happening in his own.

His horoscope and that of his betrothed's would be written on red paper and exchanged. From both households hired hands (his father was not rich enough yet to have servants) would be decked with red scarves and flowers, bringing gifts contained in glass-topped boxes. The boxes would be numbered in pairs, and the hired hands would walk in pairs, one behind the other.

The first box would contain his horoscope, and the rest gifts, ranging from silk to tea. Geese with red-dyed feathers would follow the hired hands. He often wondered why there was never music accompanying such a joyous ceremony.

His face was beaded with sweat as he trotted back and forth, balancing heavy loads of manure on a pole slung over his shoulders. No sooner had he wiped his wet face with the palm of his hand, sweat once again glistened on his brown skin, sun-stained the color of chewing tobacco. His big feet sank deep into the soft mud. The back of the heels, cracked and shrivelled like cocoons, had begun to bleed. His stomach growled. His head spun. He was hungry and tired. But he must not break for his noon meal until the sun came directly overhead, for there was still much to do. He had to flood the rice fields again, for no matter how much water he put into the earth, the growing plants seemed to soak it up like dry sponges.

When he rested for lunch, a sudden loneliness crept through him. Today he missed his brother Tse-min, who had always worked side by side with him. Alone, except for a few bugs crawling at his feet, he ate his rice and salted vegetables in haste. His tin bowl, now empty, reflected the blazing noon sun. Through watery eyes, he saw seas of growing rice plants, haloed by his tears, swaying in the warm breeze.

Although he could see other farmers taking their noon rest, he was forlorn, and felt a choking grief surging up to his throat. He started to read a book entitled *Words of Warning*, which stated that among other things, China's weakness lay in her lack of western appliances—railways, telephones, telegraphs and steamships. He read almost half of the book, and found himself suddenly content, ready to toil again in the fields until sunset.

Hoe upon his shoulder and a basket of vegetables in his hand, Tse-tung trotted home, his tired legs dragging. His heart had skipped and jumped whenever he thought of his marriage day that soon was to follow.

5

A Visit to the Temple

"The sage does not hoard his things.
The more he serves others, the more he has.
The more he gives to others, the greater his abun-
dance."   *Lao Tzu*

"If you always give, you will always have."
                                        Chinese proverb

A VISIT TO THE TEMPLE

Mao Tse-tung was putting his books in order when he heard his mother's mincing steps.

"Tse-tung, do you not like to come to the temple with me now? Your father has gone to the city on business."

"Yes Mama. But I must first finish wrapping these books for storage in the attic."

Before starting out for the temple, his mother gave rice to beggars who had come to the door. Some of them carried dying babies in their arms.

The beggars were grateful and said, "May you be blessed a thousand times, Merciful One!"

"We must share with others what we have, Tse-tung. Buddha, in his goodness, has bestowed us with plenty."

The day was brilliant but crisp. The sky was a deep blue, with puffs of white clouds lazing in the distance. Birds sang, accompanied by the rustling of falling leaves.

Half-leaning on her son, she said, "How sadly the birds sing! Especially now, that the fields are empty of growing crops." He agreed.

His mother would have gone on praying and clicking her beads if he had not gently nudged her and said, "We'd better be going before Papa finds us not about." Nodding her head, his mother smiled gently. She put her fragile arms around his big waist and tenderly drew him to her. Looking up at him she said, "You did not pray today! Why are you so restless my son?"

Before he had a chance to answer, she continued, "I know you are bothered by the sufferings and injustice around us. But be brave! Accept our misfortunes and sufferings. Do not fight it. Pray to Buddha. He will oversee us all!"

She worried about him. He no longer believed in Buddha. He thought Buddha was too passive. He told her that they must be active and fight for themselves.

He was not like ordinary sons. He had grand visions and he wanted to dedicate his life to saving his country. She knew and felt in her bones that he was going to be great. And great men, she thought, often go through grave dangers in life.

"I must come here to pray often, Tse-tung."

"Yes, Mama, you must and you will!"

But in his heart he knew that his mother would not be able to make too many trips outside the house. She was getting old. She had worked so hard and for so long that at thirty, she was physically an old woman. Every step up hill was agonizing for her. Her breathing came hard. And lately he had noticed she had to lie down more and more during the day.

"Are you ill, Mama?" he would ask. But she would bite her lips and manage a faint smile. "It's nothing. I am just a little tired. Nothing at all."

But from the paleness of her face and the shortness of her breath, he knew his mother was in pain. Yet she never uttered a word of complaint. She accepted pain, as she accepted everything else in her life, with faith and resignation. She was always tranquil, at peace with herself.

He wanted to put his long arms around his loving mother and tell her of his respect and love for her. But because he was unaccustomed to any display of affection, he could not bring himself to do it. And he was angry with himself. He wondered how long he would be able to closet all his feelings inside.

6

Wedding Day

*"The bridegroom goes in person to meet the bride.
According to the idea that regulates the relation
between the strong and the weak, the man takes the
initiative and not the woman."* Li Chi

(Book of Rites).

WEDDING DAY

Everyone, even his father, was excited. For the first time, he thought, his father seemed pleased with him. Everyone had awakened before dawn to ready the house for the auspicious occasion.

" 'Tis a day of bright sun and soft wind. A good omen for Tse-tung to take a wife," his father said excitedly.

The bridegroom went to the bride's house with two sedan chairs and a band. He was kept waiting outside the house. The bride, supported by two bridesmaids, did not come out until the band had played three times. As she climbed into the sedan chair, the band started to play again and kept on playing until they reached Mao's house in Shao Shan.

Amid fireworks and loud music and still supported by her bridesmaids, the bride stepped down from her wedding-sedan. She walked in mincing steps and pretended to look frail.

Tse-tung's feet were beginning to hurt. Unaccustomed to wearing shoes, his feet were burning now, and he felt as though he were walking on fire with little pins pricking his soles.

103

While fastening one end of a long red silk scarf to his own clothes, and the other end to the bride's clothes, he strained to see her face. He tried hard but it was no use. Her face was hidden behind her red veil. He walked backwards, and she, coming towards him, almost stumbled over the red carpet in the Mao's ancestors hall.

They bowed before the ancestors' tables. Next he bowed to her, a pledge that he would be attentive to her in the future. And then they bowed to his parents and other members of his family.

He heard his own heart thump under his ribs and the palms of his hands were damp with nervousness as he lifted his bride's veil. He still could not see her face too clearly, because from her headdress hung rows of pearls, and she kept her head bowed and her eyes lowered. But he was sure he did not like what little he could see of her features.

Her face was as round as a full moon. Her slit eyes were set a trifle too far apart, topped off by two bushy brows. Her nose was small and flat, her lips, thick and big, her mouth, wide and crooked. He grimaced at such ugliness and found himself muttering, "Aiya! A-mi-to-fu! Heavens! Mercy me!"

Then came the ceremony of touching beakers. The bride drank a sip of wine from the bridegroom's cup, while he drank a sip from hers. Thus their marriage contract was sealed.

That night, Tse-tung sat around with a heavy heart. Not even the cheerfulness of the bridal room, or the "new room" as it is customarily called, all decorated in red—red curtains, red candles, red chests of drawers, red sheets, red bedcurtains, red cushions—could lift the black cloud that shrouded his whole being.

The guests stayed long into the night and it was near dawn when the newly married couple were alone together. Without saying a word, and without removing his bridegroom gown, he went to sleep in the attic, completely ignoring his bride's presence in the bridal room below.

One week went by and he was still a stranger to his bride. In public he was cold and did not look at her or speak to her. She had not minded that, for it would not be seemly for him to notice her in the presence of others. But she was reduced to tears when he decided to leave home to stay with a friend.

Upon hearing her sobs, he stopped packing in the attic and came down to the bridal room. She rose and bowed her head, waiting for him to sit down. But he remained standing. He wrung his hands and seemed to have difficulty in expressing what he had in mind to tell her.

He told her to sit down and looking past her, he said, "Please understand, and I beg you not to take it amiss. I am young still, and have no desire to take a wife just now. Our fathers have forced us into this."

She did not fully understand his position. But there was so much sympathy in his eyes that she felt comforted.

She wanted to thank him aloud but she bit her lips and remained silent, for it would not be seemly for her to say so many words.

She knew he did not like her looks, but he had enough grace not to say it to her face, and for that she was forever grateful. Her sadness was lightened by the thought that although she had lost a husband, she had indeed gained a friend.

Mao Tse-tung again antagonized his father by not consummating the marriage that his father had arranged for him.

7

Leaving Home

*"When wings are grown, children and birds will fly
away."* Chinese Proverb

*"The son may not go abroad while his parents are
alive. If he goes abroad, he must have a fixed place
to which he goes."* Analect

LEAVING HOME

Between father and son the tension worsened with the passing of each day. The young Mao's grievance against his father was compounded by his grievance against the foreigners humiliating China. He was also indignant over the Emperor's inability to withstand foreign invasion. Foreign troops occupied the capital of Peking and other great coastal cities. Though not entirely subjugated, China was constantly being humiliated. Notices of 'Dogs and Chinese not admitted' were put up in the park of the Shanghai Bund.

The collapse of the Hundred Days Reform gave the reactionaries full power. Their antiforeign feeling intensified. Many officials channeled economic, social and political discontent against the foreigners. Antiforeign secret societies, encouraged by court reactionaries and provincial governors, were formed to combat foreign aggression. Chief among these societies was the Boxers, who began to attack foreigners.

By 1900, numerous Chinese Christians and foreigners were killed in the North. On June 1, 450 marines were added to detachments guarding the Peking legations. The Boxers, who believed this was a prelude to foreign invasion, destroyed the Peking-Tientsin Railroad connections. They declared war on all foreigners when reinforcements, under British Admiral Seymour, were sent to Peking on June 11, 1900. When the Seymour expedition was driven back to Tientsin, a larger naval expedition stormed the Taku forts. The Chinese counterattacked the foreign legations at Peking, and the empress Dowager ordered the extermination of all aliens in China.

On August 14, 1901, the international armies relieved the besieged legations of Peking, and the imperial court fled to Shensi Province. China was forced to secure peace on humiliating terms.

After the Boxer Rebellion, the Empress Dowager at last recognized the need for reform. Until her death in 1908, she fostered the reforms that she previously opposed. Among the important reforms introduced in 1901 were the educational reforms. A ministry of education was established and a comprehensive education program called for establishment in the provinces of western-style education, from kindergarten to college. In 1905 the civil service examinations were abolished and study abroad was encouraged. The United States further stimulated this program by returning part of the Boxer indemnity in 1907 to support Chinese students studying abroad.

"Why is he not pleased?" Mao's father was again scolding him in front of his mother, "Now that we have twenty-two mou of good land and a thriving grain transport and selling business?"

"But Jen-shen, Tse-tung is not like the others. He is not happy just tilling the soil. He wishes to attend a place of learning at Hsiang Hsiang," his mother interceded for him.

"Hsiang Hsiang! That's fifty li away. A boy at sixteen should think of having sons to warm his father's old bones! And it will also cost me 1400 coppers for five months' board, lodging and books! No! No! There is no end to that boy's spending!"

Weeks passed and there were more quarrels between father and son. Finally the father relented.

And so, when the markets were again filled with orange mountains of persimmons and from the northern hills now covered with fallen leaves of red and gold, came gusts of chilling wind, Tse-tung, feeling sad and happy at the same time, packed his few belongings in bundles and tied them to a bamboo pole.

The next morning, bundles slung over his shoulders, he set out on his journey to Hsiang Hsiang. He wore the blue cotton tunic and trousers that his mother had mended and cleaned the night before. His sunburnt face was solemn, his hair washed and his pigtail freshly braided. "I look almost a man!" he thought as he walked away from the terraced fields and pine-covered ridges, in his slow, massive, but easy movements so unlike the quick, sharp steps of most Hunan peasants in his region.

Three times he turned around and waved to his mother whose eyes were filled with tears.

"I am saddened by his going," his mother said to Tse-min who was wiping his own eyes with the edge of his sleeves.

She walked awkwardly back to his room. There was a heaviness, a lack of liveliness in her step.

The room was small, like the one she shared with her husband, yet it suddenly seemed large and empty now. Her footsteps echoed as she went around cleaning and dusting. She pushed open the window, and saw two lotus-filled ponds directly below, and beyond them acres of fields now empty of growing crops, looked gaunt and desolate. A lump came into her throat. "His going leaves emptiness in my heart," she thought.

Though he had confided in her less and less as he grew older, he was to her like the sun. And like the plants in the fields, she wondered if she might not die without sunshine in her heart.

8

Journey on Foot to a Place of Learning

"Learn to handle a writing brush, and you will never handle a begging bowl."   *Chinese proverb*

JOURNEY ON FOOT TO A PLACE OF LEARNING

Young Mao walked toward the direction of Hsiang Hsiang by way of the temple he had visited with his mother when he was a child. It was empty and he went inside. All around him, it was void, empty, dead, like his own heart.

From the mountain where the temple stood, he noticed for the first time how low his house lay in the narrow ravine, sandwiched between two mountains. At the sight of his house which was roofed partially with round grey tiles and partially with thatch, he felt a sudden longing to return home.

Already he missed his mother, his brothers, and his sister. They had much love for each another. Tears misted his eyes, veiling everything around him except a barren tree that stood solitarily outside the temple. He felt lonely and barren as the solitary tree. A chaos of emotion came over him and he resumed his journey.

As he neared Hsiang Hsiang, he stopped by the roadside and wrote a letter to his mother, telling her he would come home to visit her often. Then he wrote another letter to his brothers and sister. He told them that someday he would fetch all of them to come to Hsiang Hsiang to study. Later, he thought, they might even be able to attend schools in the provincial capital of Changsha together.

After revealing his plans to his family, he felt his sadness slowly evaporating. All at once he felt liberated, restful and free. The night was almost perfect except for a few clouds scudding by, darkening the silvery moonlight intermittently. The leaves spiraled down from the trees in the mellow night air.

He head a dog bark in the next valley. Somewhere near a pond, the last of the summer cicadas sang. Soon a field sparrow joined in with his melancholic whistling.

Mao's heart pulsated to the rhythm of the sparrow's song, slowly at first then faster and faster. He heard the croaking of frogs. A field mouse darted in front of him. He reached out for the little creature. "Stay, little one!" Quick as a flash, the mouse darted out of sight. And he was again alone under an immense sky.

When dawn came and the pink clouds in the eastern horizon began gently to beget a new day, his spirit soared higher and higher, over Shao Shan, over Hsiang Hsiang, over Changsha . . .

He was happy and felt like a star that could rotate all by itself in its own firmament.

9

Awkward Newcomer

"When one is with true friends even water drunk together is sweet enough."   *Chinese proverb*

AWKWARD NEWCOMER

When the sixteen-year-old Mao arrived at the school in Hsiang Hsiang, the gate-keeper was reluctant to let him in.

Eyeing Mao surreptitiously, the gate-keeper said, "Hey, this is a school for refined, well-dressed little boys. What business have you here, country-bumpkin? I have not heard of the school master's talk of hiring a laborer for the school ground!"

"I—" the young Mao stuttered meekly, "I have permission to attend this school." Mao swallowed his anger and his pride in order that he might attend this school where new knowledge of the west was being taught.

He found his place in the school despite this upsetting beginning. Shortly after his arrival he made many friends, among them the two Siao brothers, Emile Siao and Siao-yu.

He did very well in school and continued with his voluminous reading. He was well liked by his teachers for his ambitious nature and his fervent patriotism.

Like his rich young class-mates, Mao too dreamed of great deeds. He, too, wanted to lead armies and build up China!

After a year, Mao became dissatisfied with the provincial school in Hsiang Hsiang. With his friend Emile Siao, he walked to Changsha, the capital city of Hunan Province, where he enrolled as a student at the secondary modern school.

Changsha, like the whole of China, was in a revolutionary ferment. Here, Mao read a newspaper for the first time in his life. His greatest hero then was Sun Yat-sen, the founder of the Chinese Republic. To Mao, Sun was a master of the new knowledge of the West.

Mao wrote an article urging Sun Yat-sen to return from abroad to become the first president of the Chinese Republic, and pasted it on the school wall. This was Mao's first venture in journalism.

When Mao was eighteen years old, he cut off his pigtail to show his scorn for the past and for the Manchu dynasty that had ruled China for more than two hundred years.

Like most of his contemporaries, Mao thought that the millions and millions of peasants for ages had been exploited by the luxury-loving, debauched Imperial administrators and by bad landlords.

Mao aired his thoughts to his friends: "Our culture and the creative genius of our people have been bound for ages and deformed, like the feet of

120

Chinese girls, by the princes, the scholar bureau-crats and their gentry, none of whom ever did any useful work.

"The keepers of Confucian traditions are forever writing delicate poetry! They enjoy their exquisite surroundings and feast on good food! They debauch themselves with their concubines! Of course these cultivated gentlemen abhor any thought of change and development. But change we must! We must free the millions and millions of peasants who have been chained for thousands of years by abject poverty!

"We must free women from their slavery! We must reform our family system, which, like the whole of China, is a prison! Equal ownership of land! Freedom for women! Down with the Manchu government! Set China free!"

On October 9, 1911, a bomb exploded in Wuch'ang with the slogan, 'Set China Free!' Cities fell like ripe plums, into the hands of rebels for democracy. Sun Yat-sen was recalled from America, and was elected provisional president of the Chinese Republic. However, the Imperial Manchu Government still resisted in Peking.

Mao joined the National Army and saw with pride the white *Han* flag raised in many military gover-nors' headquarters.

On February 12, 1912, the Manchu Emperor

121

abdicated and the Chinese Republic was established.

Mao resigned from the army and returned to Changsha.

10

Year of Indecision

"Learn as though you might not be attaining your object and were always fearing lest you miss it."
Analects

YEAR OF INDECISION

At nineteen, Mao's revolutionary fervor gave way when he registered in quick succession for many possibilities of study in Changsha. He entered a police academy, a soap-making school, a law school, a business school and then a higher commercial school run by the government.

Mao stayed only for a month at the commercial school because all the lessons were in English and he did not think he could learn the language fast enough to keep up.

Next, he tried the First Provincial Middle School where he stayed for six months, but then decided to educate himself.

Mao was sitting on the steps of the Hunan Provincial Library, next to a pile of books that he had borrowed from the library. His cotton gown was threadbare and no match for the cool morning breeze. Rubbing his hands furiously to keep warm, he exhaled, forming trails of steam that floated upwards, and danced in front of his blurry eyes. His stomach growled for want of food.

He reached into his pocket and took out two shiny copper coins, the last of his savings. Slowly he walked over to a street vendor who was shouting his wares on top of his lungs: "Rice cakes and soybean curd for sale! Delicious and nutritious! Come and buy delicious rice cakes and soybean curd!"

Before Mao even opened his mouth, the vendor handed him two rices cakes saying, "Same thing, sir, today?" And turning to his other customers, the vendor bragged, "See, this young gentleman likes my rice cakes so much that he has been buying two from me every day for the past six months!"

Wanting to humor the good vendor, Mao nodded and smiled as he paid the vendor with the last of his copper coins.

His stomach growled again. This time it ached with throbbing pangs. The two rices cakes felt wonderfully warm against the palm of his hand. He carefully unwrapped one and started to munch it gingerly. He was still hungry when he finished savoring the last mouthful of it. He so wanted to eat the other, but he put an extra wrapping on the remaining rice cake and put it in his pocket. The aroma was too tempting!

"Ops!" he muttered, "A big hole in this pocket!" He caught the rice cake in the nick of time as it was dropping out of the pocket. He checked his left pocket carefully before putting the rice cake in it.

126

"To think I almost lost my lunch and supper!" he murmured. Laden with books, he was the first to enter when the librarian opened the door of the library.

"Good morning young man! Let me help you carry some of those books!" the librarian, a kindly old man, greeted Mao. "I have a map of the world to show you this morning, Mr. Mao, before I hang it up on the wall. It just came this morning."

The librarian spread the large map on his desk and Mao studied it methodically. With his index finger, he traced the boundaries of the major countries, starting from China and then up to Russia, over to Canada and then down to the United States of America.

"Surprised to find that the Middle Kingdom is not the largest in the world, Mr. Mao?" the librarian asked the awe-struck Mao who was getting very excited, seeing a world map for the first time in his life.

Pointing to Russia and the United States, Mao said, "Yes, these are all great powers and Russia is much larger than China and the United States is large too, with rich natural resources and yet both are much less populated than China." There was a slight touch of disappointment in his voice.

After helping the librarian nail the map to the library wall, Mao just stood there as if transfixed.

Then he sighed, "Aiya! China is not the center of the world!"

The librarian thanked him and said, "I am afraid I don't have anymore great books here for you. You have read practically every important book we have in the library for the past six months! Tell me, Mr. Mao, what are you going to do next?"

"I was thinking of going to The First Normal College here in Changsha, sir. I want to be a teacher." He paused, then continued sadly, "but my father has cut off my allowance ever since he found out I left school and have no regular employment."

"Why don't you write your father again to let him know of your present plans to attend school! I am a father myself and I know all fathers are more than glad to give financial support toward their sons' education as long as they are able to afford it," the librarian advised Mao paternally.

So Mao made up his mind to write to his father, asking for his consent and support. Although Mao despised his father and all that his father stood for— the family system, the source of all China's ills, he believed—he saw no other way to a higher education.

"I'm a rotten pragmatist at heart!" Mao thought, and chuckled to himself as he humbly but reluctantly wrote his father in a respectful manner.

11

Murmurings from a Discontented Father

"If your sons are bad, should you keep money?
But if your sons are good, do you need money?"
                                    Chinese proverb

"It is easier to rule a nation than it is to rule a son."
                                    Chinese proverb

MURMURINGS FROM A
DISCONTENTED FATHER

Mao Jen-sheng, my grandfather, was in a good mood the day his oldest son's letter arrived. He had just made a huge profit from his grain business.

"Aiya! Is there no end to spending in this house!" he said to his wife. "There seems to be no end to spending, with you and your Number One son! He is now in the capital city of Changsha and wants to attend some useless school called Changsha First Normal College." He waved his son's letter at his wife. "There is no telling what that impudent son of yours is doing in Changsha. People tell me violent battles are being fought there between the forces of Old Confucian China and the followers of democracy."

"Did he not say what he is learning?" his wife asked.

"Probably some more of that useless modern junk his head is already filled with!" Mao Jen-sheng answered in disgust.

"Is he well and how about his place of stay?" the gentle wife asked with maternal concern.

"We are to write him at one of his teacher's—erh—yes—here." He squinted a little and adjusted his spectacles, "Yang Ch'ang-chi by name!" Then he stooped over his frail wife and whispered, but loud enough for his other two sons and daughter to hear, "Maybe this teacher has a pretty daughter Tse-tung is interested in, eh!"

His wife was relieved by the half-serious, half-joking manner with which he conveyed to her that everything was well with her Number One son.

She walked away quickly and for the first time since her son's departure, there was a liveliness in her step. Left alone and unobserved, she cried in relief as though tears were the only pleasures she had left.

In the three years since her oldest son's departure, she had worried about him and prayed constantly to Buddha that one day he would come back safely to her and the family. Life went on, day following day, season following season, and she forever waited for her oldest son to return. She thought that until *he* actually told her that he would definitely not come back, all would be well and bearable for her. But it was not.

The strain of waiting damaged her already ravaged body, putting fresh lines in her face where the flesh became wrinkled and sagged. And around her eyes and mouth there were deep creases not set there by sun and wind but by tears of loneliness.

"Aiya! Maybe Tse-tung will never come back!"
Whereupon, she took up her beads and started to
pray again.

"The unfilial one writes only when he is need of
money!" Mao Jen-sheng sneered. But in his heart he
was pleased with his oldest son's decision to become
a teacher.

Shortly afterwards he sent a large sum of money to
the Changsha First Normal College for his son's
tuition and board.

12

A New School,
an Enlightened Teacher

"A good teacher is better than a barrowful of books."
                                        Chinese proverb.

*"Teachers may open the door but you must enter by
  yourself."*   *Chinese proverb*

*"Although gold has its price, learning is beyond
  price."*   *Chinese proverb*

A NEW SCHOOL,
AN ENLIGHTENED TEACHER

The spring rain had lashed through the city of Changsha, and it was unusually fresh and sparkling this Sunday morning. The sparrows, which had disappeared during winter, were chirping again on the branches of a cherry tree outside Mao Tse-tung's window.

"Ah, the first song of spring! How lovely!" he thought. The bird's chirping stirred him gently, plucking a string in his young heart. Instead of joining the Siao brothers for calisthenics as he did about this time every morning, he decided to just sit by the window, looking and listening for signs of spring.

Lately, his moods had fluctuated greatly. One moment he would be elated because he liked Changsha's First Normal College. He enjoyed the courses he was taking and the intellectual stimulation provided by the faculty members and students at the school.

For Mao, his ethics teacher, Professor Yang Ch'ang-chi stood out above all the others.

Yang, a philosophical idealist, had studied at various universities in Europe and was a patriotic man of great integrity. He was always kind and generous to his students.

The feeling of admiration was mutual between him and Mao. Under Yang, Mao wrote some of his best essays. One, entitled "The Energy of the Mind", written for Yang's ethics course, so impressed the teacher, that he marked the paper one hundred plus five.

But Mao felt downtrodden, hopeless, recalling Professor Yang's exhortation in class. "China needs new ways! China needs new blood! She is dying!"

Invariably he felt pessimistic, helpless. He wanted to have an important part in strengthening and reforming China which was weakening at the hands of exploiters from within and without, but thought it was a hopeless wish.

"Tse-tung!" one of the Siao brothers called as he came into the room, "Why are you still sitting there in your night clothes? We'll be late for brunch at the Yangs. I wouldn't miss it for the world! Mrs. Yang always cooks such delicious meals! And instead of Professor Yang's only son, his only daughter, K'ai-hui, will be there today!"

Mao was in a serious mood and ignored his friend's small talk, as he dressed slowly and absent-mindedly.

On the way to Professor Yang's house in the city, Mao walked leisurely a few paces behind the Siao brothers. Spring came early in the outskirts of Changsha City, bringing with it plum blossoms white as snow. For as far as Mao's eyes could see, pink cherry blooms marched softly over the gentle slopes of the lower hills, where farmers were busy planting seeds for their rice crops. The song of birds hung in the air. Since coming to Changsha, this was the first time he had been aware of the birds, as if the warm sunrise of this spring morning were needed to make him hear them sing. He closed his eyes and took in a deep breath, and let himself be caressed by the young day. The Siao brothers were still talking about Professor Yang's daughter, Yang K'ai-hui.

"She is a very pretty girl!" Siao Yu said.

"And very intelligent too!" Emile exclaimed. "But," he continued, "she is extremely progressive and has westernized mannerisms that she picked up as a child, living abroad with her parents. She speaks and reads several European languages including English, German and Spanish."

At the mention of Professor Yang's daughter's ability to speak and read foreign languages, Mao's curiosity was aroused.

"I have never met anyone of my own age who lived abroad," Mao thought silently, "let alone somebody who actually reads and speaks another language than Chinese! Just think the wealth of knowledge in western books she has at her disposal!" He strained hard to hear more of the Siao brothers' conversation.

Mao heard Siao Yu say reproachfully, "From what I hear, she even uses incomprehensible foreign jargon when she jokes and argues with Professor Yang. Imagine, a daughter arguing and joking with her honorable father!"

"She doesn't like to do housework either!" Emile said.

"Well," Siao Yu sighed, "how can one expect her to do the cooking, cleaning and washing when she is so busy heading some nonsensical movement that agitates for the equality of women!"

"Isn't she only about seventeen?" Emile asked.

"Yes, but she is quite mature for her age and she is planning to enter the university next year," Siao Yu replied. "I wonder how she is going to like us, the three poorest, biggest country bumpkins from way back where!" Emile said jokingly and then he turned around expecting to hear some kind of reply from Mao. But Mao pretended not to hear. Inhaling deeply, Siao Yu said, "I am starved!"

"So am I," Emile chimed in, "I hope Mrs. Yang and not her daughter, is preparing the main dishes!"

"I imagine Mrs. Yang makes her daughter help her with the housework regardless how much the young lady dislikes domestic chores. From what I can see, Mrs. Yang is a very strict mother and would not let her daughter get away with any of her childish nonsense!"

"Professor Yang's daughter must be quite different from all the other girls I've met in Changsha!" thought Mao. From what little he could gather from the Siao brothers' conversation, Mao felt that Yang K'ai-hui would be most interesting to have as a friend and though he refused to admit it to himself, he was beginning to feel anxious about meeting her.

13

An Old-Fashioned Mother
and
a Modern Daughter

"The woman must follow the man. In youth she follows her father and elder brother. In marriage she follows her husband. When widowed, she follows her son." Li Chi   *(Book of Rites)*

AN OLD-FASHIONED MOTHER
AND A MODERN DAUGHTER

All morning Yang K'ai-hui was busy helping her mother prepare dinner. It had seemed like an eternity, with the endless cutting and chopping of meat and vegetables. She had no patience with any kind of housework.

"Oh Mama! Does it really matter whether I cut these pork strips into $1/3$ inch or $1/8$ inch? Pork is pork. After it's cooked, it all tastes the same."

But to her consternation, her mother had made sure she cut every pork strip to a uniform size of $1/8$ inch. Later, she demurred when she had to help her mother clean house.

"Mama, if we clean this house once more, it is going to smell antiseptic, like a hospital."

"Men folks appreciate fine food and an orderly house, K'ai-hui. It's the best way to please them!"

"But I don't think it is necessary to please a man just that way. I want to please him by sharing his work, his goals in life, his ambition. I want to please him just being myself, free to make my own decisions in matters of mutual concern." She looked sideways at her mother and then added, "Anyway, too much pleasing on one side makes a very lop-sided marriage!"

Seeing how submissive her mother was to her father in all things, she felt it her duty to disagree. Lately it had also seemed for her a matter of course to contradict her parents. Unconsciously, torrents of words would just flow out of her mouth.

"Mama, loving Papa doesn't mean you have to give up your identity."

"But I am happy, K'ai-hui. Your father is loving and he is just. And I am giving myself to caring for the ones I love best in the world. What more can a woman ask out of life?"

For most women living in China today, not much —that's for sure!" K'ai-hui said sarcastically. "Especially peasant women. Their work is the hardest there is. Even the livestock receives better care! The women do the cooking and housekeeping. They take care of animals, go to the well for water, raise children, work in the fields, trotting back and forth balancing heavy loads of manure, vegetables or straw on their shoulders. In their mid-twenties, they are old women.

"If the man is not happy, he beats them. If he is rich, he installs concubines in his bed. Women can ask a great deal more out of life, Mama!"

She stopped her meat-cutting and continued, getting more excited by the minute. "We must ask men to treat us as individuals. We must demand equality in education. We must be able to contribute our brain-power to work toward a better society. We must be able to share their work and to reap the fruits of this joint effort equally."

"You are talking like a foreign devil, daughter!" Her mother tried in vain to change the subject.

Ignoring her mother's remark, K'ai-hui went on. "When the time comes, my man will have to accept me as an equal, not a subordinate."

"You'll have a long long wait for such a man, daughter!" Her mother winked at her and smiled.

"I'll wait forever if necessary!"

"You are still a little girl, K'ai-hui. In a few years, you'll feel differently. You'll get married and settled down, like the rest of us!"

For a fleeting moment, the young woman thought it wonderful that her mother still regarded her as her little girl. She felt safe and warm under her mother's protective wings. Yet she felt hurt that her mother should take her so lightly, thinking all her ideas were but little girls' nonsense. She was surprised that one who loved her so much should understand her so little.

She no longer regarded herself young. She was seventeen and would be entering the University of Peking next year. She hoped her mother would not object to her wanting to leave home and live in the dormitory where she could be more independent.

Though her mother was in every way a docile wife, she was a strict mother. Well, K'ai-hui knew she had better not cross her! Less solicitous than before, K'ai-hui resumed her tedious chore of meat cutting.

Her father came quietly behind her, and slapping her on the rear, he said, "I overheard every word you said to Mama just now. I always knew my lovely daughter had a naughty streak in her!"

"Ouch Papa! You mustn't do that, now that I am a young lady of seventeen. Mama would think it improper. Besides, what would people say?"

"Since when do you care what others say, daughter! And don't you ever change either, for that's what makes us Yangs unique."

"Unique enough so Mama will let me join in the conversation at table this afternoon?"

"Impossible! That's outside my jurisdiction! You'll have to clear it with Mama!"

"You are just saying that. You know Mama always does what you tell her. Despite all your modern ideas, you still want to keep women in their place!" she sneered. "But I still love you, you old rascal, you bit of a noodle!" She hugged her father and kissed him on both cheeks, and quickly added that 'noodle' in her vocabulary had a nuance of affection in it.

Her father shook his head. "If I allow you to participate, K'ai-hui, my students won't stand a chance! Incidentally, I am inviting a new student, a friend of the Siao brothers, to come today."

"Who is he?" K'ai-hui asked.

"His name is Mao Tse-tung and he is a farmer's son from Shao Shan."

"Oh! Since when does Changsha's First Normal College admit yokels?" she asked mischievously.

"He's a farmer's son, but he is no country bumpkin! He has a very brilliant and logical mind and his essays are excellent. He's the best in my ethics class. I hope I can convince him to enroll in my philosophy and psychology classes as well."

"He might write brilliant essays, Papa, but I bet when he opens his mouth to talk, nobody can understand him." She chuckled and mimicked the lowly Hunan dialect. "His accent doesn't really sound too different from the rest of us Hunanese," her father said cryptically.

K'ai-hui brushed her long hair from her delicate face, shrugged, and walked swiftly away.

Her father watched her, loving the grace with which she walked. Small and delicate, she was perfectly proportioned. Too stubborn and militant for a woman! "But so beautiful and bright, this daughter of mine!" Professor Yang thought with fatherly pride.

14

When Young Eyes Meet

"When there is too much talk, beware of trouble.

*When there is too much food, beware of indiges-
tion."*
         Chinese Proverb

"'I heard' is good, but 'I saw' is better."
         Chinese proverb

WHEN YOUNG EYES MEET

"How very boring! I'll have to sit through another long dinner. I wonder if Papa's students ever get indigestion from the heated debates, and the spicy hot pepper dishes that are Mama's specialties," thought K'ai-hui as she and her mother entered the dining room. Her head was bowed low.

She recognized the Siao brothers, Emile and Siao Yu, who had been to her house before. They remained seated. But the new one, Mao Tse-tung, stood up and bowed to her mother.

Out of the corners of her eyes, she saw that he was very tall. Since she was petite and since her head was still bowed low, she could only see his hands which were white and soft, with very long sensitive fingers. He was carrying carefully wrapped packages of newspapers and books. The bottom half of his long grey cotton gown looked old and worn.

She was relieved that he had not spoken, for she felt giddy, and would surely die laughing if she heard his peasant accent. What if he smelled of cow dung? She did not exactly think of it in a degrading way. Being the daughter of an intellectual, she was

153

ignorant about ways of the peasants. She had always associated farmers with dirt, mud and cow manure.

She was glad that Mao Tse-tung had taken the seat directly opposite her. If she could not take part in the conversation, she could at least observe this new student of whom her father had talked so highly.

Above the frayed collar of the grey gown was a face both sensual and intellectual. His eyes were large, wide and penetrating. His chin was strong, with a prominent mole. His jet black hair, though not in queue, was thick and long. She also liked his high-bridged nose and prominent cheek bones. His thick eyebrows and domed forehead gave an impression of strength and dedication.

"And what a sensual mouth!" K'ai-hui thought, her pearly white face blushing a little. "His teeth are so white and even; his smile so charming!" She couldn't imagine that he was not genuinely sincere in what he was saying.

She was so busy studying him that she had not followed the main conversation. She caught a few things here and there and then only when they concerned Mao.

"Tse-tung, tell me what western books you have read lately," her father asked. Very unsure of himself, Mao answered in short, halting sentences. But his accent wasn't as noticeable as she had anticipated.

154

Mao said, "I've read Chinese translations of T.H. Huxley's *Evolution and Ethics,* John Stuart Mill's *On Liberty,* Adam Smith's *The Wealth of Nations,* Darwin's *Origin of the Species.*"

Nodding his head in approval, her father said, "Yes, I've read the marginal notes you made on Friedrich Paulsen's *System of Ethics.*"

"Yes," Mao replied, "I've written 12,000 characters in all, Professor Yang."

"Good, Tse-tung, it shows you have a firm grasp of the subject. In my courses, I try to emphasize two major themes: individual autonomy and self-realization and responsibility to society." Her father swallowed another mouthful of rice and continued. "I'm glad you are socially oriented and have joined the Changsha Student Association already, Tse-tung. You must also meet some of the other revolutionary-minded students, Liu Shao-ch'i, Jen Pi-shih, Li Li-san and Ts'ai Ho-sen, if you have not already done so."

"Yes, Professor Yang. Tsai Ho-sen and I are also thinking of organizing a more disciplined student organization dedicated to strengthening China through strengthening Chinese youth." Mao paused and glanced at K'ai-hui. "It will be called the New People's Study Society," Mao stammered. "We are holding our first meeting next week. And if Miss Yang would like to attend this meeting, she'll be most welcome." Mao blushed. He felt terribly ashamed of a trifle like that, and of his little slip in speech.

Yang K'ai-hui, too, was at a loss for words and for the first time in her life she was glad that she wasn't expected to say anything. She blushed as she poured tea for everyone at the table. Mao thought every movement of her hands was as delicately graceful as the sweep of a sea gull's wings.

For the rest of the meal, K'ai-hui was flustered, but she did not ignore Mao. She communicated with her eyes. And when their visions met, she smiled at him.

She thought that his searching eyes, for a brief moment, had held her in his affection. Her heart took wings and fluttered.

That night she was pensive and less talkative. She spent most of her free time in her room thinking about Mao. She thought he was almost too austerely earnest. How tightly he closed his well-molded lips when he listened! But all the greater the contrast, when his eyes suddenly softened and a boyishly enthusiastic smile lit up his face!

"K'ai-hui, you are in love!" she told herself. "Impossible, I'm not that impetuous to go for that 'love at first sight' rubbish! Really now, what has Mao got to arouse such tender feelings in me! True, he is earnest, but in some ways, he is rather prosaic.

But how else can I explain this strong desire to see him again? Perhaps this is just a seventeen-year-old's infatuation for an older man of nineteen! It will soon pass!"

But the thirst in her heart could not be quenched. His appearance is in no way unusual, K'ai-hui thought, and yet something about him, something of the simple peasant, singled him out from the rest of Papa's more sophisticated, city-bred students.

She decided she must see him before next week's meeting lest she languish.

15

Awakening of a Young Man's Heart

"One cannot clap with only one hand."
                                    Chinese proverb

*"He who loves hunting and women abandons his
    state to ruin."* Li Chi   *(Book of Rites)*

"The scholar keeps himself free from all stain."
  Li Chi   *(Book of Rites)*

AWAKENING OF A YOUNG MAN'S HEART

When Mao and the Siao brothers returned to their dormitory from the Yangs, Mao immediately slipped into his own room like a fugitive, and sat staring at his books, feeling utterly downcast. He did not want the Siao brothers to question him about his impression of Yang K'ai-hui. Though meeting her was an exciting experience, it was nevertheless an ordeal for him. The strain of being polite and being on guard all day lest he should appear foolish before such an intelligent girl as K'ai-hui, bound him with invisible cords till his head ached with pounding discomfort.

He wanted to forget her, but he found he could not. When he tried to remember how she had looked, it was like groping in a dream. Yet when he closed his eyes, a sharp image drifted up . . . A delicate face in the style of an ancient Chinese painting, with black hair. Almond-shaped black eyes sparkled under clear-cut, arched eyebrows. So exquisite was the entire outline that it gave him a curious feeling of coldness. Even the somewhat uneven lips seemed

161

carved out of coral from the icy depths of the oceans! But when those lips parted charmingly to allow a glimpse of lovely teeth, the smile softened the whole image, and a tinge of color came into the pearly white face. The carved figure turned into a beautiful young woman!

Mao liked Yang K'ai-hui's delicate smallness, her quickness at walking, talking and laughing, her oval-shaped face, her narrow nose, the tip of which turned pertly upwards. Much to his dismay, he had even noticed such details as freckles on her nose and cheeks. Slim and lithe, she's graceful as a sylph! Mao, nibbling at his pencil, was lost in thought. As he tried to shut out the very first moment when she smiled at him and something at once mischievous and passionate sparked in her deep dark eyes, he felt saddened and lost. How much worse, even, then the sadness he felt as a child in his mother's arms, when he saw the moon eclipsed and the world was for a brief moment in semi-darkness!

Closing his book, the pages of which he had not turned for over an hour, Mao got up from his desk and went to the window and watched the moon rise over the mountain. Insects sang, and a fresh breeze carried the scent and murmur of the village across the fields. He saw that the cottage of the schoolmaster was still glowing. The light shone on the lotus pond in front of it, making the dimly white flowers more visible and brighter in the moonlight. The leaves, beaded with moisture from a late afternoon shower, appeared to be specked with tiny precious gems, and remained perfectly still in the calm spring night. Sunk in the deepest and most confusing thoughts, he stood there gazing at the moon, which seemed to have diminished a little further. And as he gazed, the moon and flowers vanished and there were only the white shapes floating in the pond.

It's not because I am not interested in her, Mao reasoned to himself, it is the circumstances.

Contrary to the tranquility he felt now as he stood gazing at the moon while the village slept in delightful silence, the world around him was in turmoil. There were draughts in the northwestern regions of the country. Millions were dying from starvation. Everywhere peasants were suppressed and exploited by their landlords. Tyrannical warlords ruled the provinces with iron hands, freely chaining and executing those who dared raise a voice against them. Everywhere, students were restless, eager for reforms.

"Times are too critical and the need for knowledge too urgent for me to spend time in romantic reveries. I've much to do for my fellowmen!" Mao reminded himself. "Besides, Yang K'ai-hui has been to so many places and seen so many things, why would she be interested in a farmer's son? Her family is so far above mine, I doubt she even remembers my name after today."

Mao sagged against the window-sill. He made up his mind not to seek any closer relationship with Yang K'ai-hui beyond that of a friend. "It's not my own choice," he thought sadly, "I am only reconciling myself to what has to be!" Pleased by his logic, he almost believed that he had never been attracted to Yang K'ai-hui, and, even if he had, he could easily free himself from any further romantic involvement with her.

Out of habit, he read until he fell asleep.

Writings of Hegel and Marx crowded the little night stand next to his bed.

16

A Walk in the Country

"Sorrow is the child of too much joy."
                                        Chinese proverb

A WALK IN THE COUNTRY

When Yang K'ai-hui left her father's office, after leading a three-hour discussion of equal rights for women, she met Mao coming out of the school library. His arms were laden with books and pamphlets. The two Siao brothers were with him.

"We were just going for a walk in the country, would you care to join us Miss Yang?" Emile asked.

Upon seeing her, Mao seemed nervous. He was less in command of himself than usual. He tripped over a pebble and fell with one hand on the ground, his books and pamphlets scattering all over the school yard. He was stiff and sullen. After a brief greeting, he did not attempt to participate in the conversations.

K'ai-hui sensed that Mao was putting a broad river between them, a river which boat or raft was forbidden to cross. So, after a while, she walked silently with Emile, a few paces behind Mao and Siao Yu.

The sky was of the clearest blue suffused with pink, limpid and luminous. The warm weather had brought out hordes of butterflies and bees. In groups they flew from flower to flower. In the stillness of the countryside, seemingly theirs were the only activities in the spreading and generating of life.

K'ai-hui observed Mao's movements which were relaxed, but at the same time deliberate. Some of his manners were arrogant, cold. At times he seemed not to notice her at all. Yet, it was this seeming coldness and apathy in him, a person obviously romantic and responsive, that attracted her. And now she wondered if ever she might be able to capture the spring of warmth and affection that were sometimes discernible in his eyes and his smiles.

Minutes ticked away. Suddenly, Mao turned to Siao Yu and said, "We youths and the intelligensia in China must unite and work hard for reforms. More action, less talk. Talk without action is less useful than cow dung. At least cow dung can be used as fertilizer while talk cannot."

Although K'ai-hui thought him crude to bring up the subject of cow dung in front of her, she liked his sharp metaphors. He had the ability to speak his mind in clear, simple, vivid words.

"If we want to begin our group activities," Mao continued, "we should be prepared to give ourselves wholeheartedly. Aside from hardships and frustrations, we are in constant danger of being arrested by the government."

"I'm fully aware of what it entails, Tse-tung!"

Siao Yu retorted. "Right now, I'm in the process of setting up a discussion group. It will be a reading-discussion session."

"Books are legless. We can open and shut them at will!" Mao interrupted. "It's easier for us to read and talk about our problems than it is to slaughter a pig. When we want to catch a pig, it will run. When we want to slaughter it, it will squeal!"

"But don't you think some of us are rather young and inexperienced and need to gain knowledge from books and discussions before we can formulate a course of action?" Siao Yu said.

"But see to it we don't go on reading and debating forever, Mr. Siao!" Mao retorted. Quick to perceive nuances in Siao Yu's remarks, Mao showed his incandescent temper with a sarcastic but infectious laugh. Soon the three friends were laughing. And K'ai-hui heard her own laughter like an echo. She despised herself for joining in, for letting Mao think she was so easily amused by his remarks. When they stopped laughing, Emile was the first to speak.

"I'm sorry to change the subject, but do you think we have enough money to buy pork for next week?"

"Why are we wasting time worrying about ordinary matters of daily life!" Mao replied impatiently. "If we don't have pork, we can always eat rice and vegetables." Turning to K'ai-hui, Mao asked, "What do you think Miss Yang?"

K'ai-hui shrugged and said nothing. She did not want to take sides. But at that moment, the simplicity, dignity, zeal and naivete in Mao, an uncomplicated peasant, walked out of books and became as real to her as the rice she ate.

Mao preferred to talk of large matters. Such subjects as the nature of man, of human society, of China, of the world, of the universe, usually brought a quizzical beam to his eyes.

After her walk in the country, Yang became more melancholy. She tried to erase Mao from her romantic daydreams.

"He's so self-contained and so intent upon remaining a mere visitor in my heart," she thought despairingly. Yet she could not keep him out of her mind. This morning she felt stuffed, unable to eat.

"K'ai-hui, you have been picking at your food for days now. What ails you, daughter?" Her mother was worried.

"You are imagining things again, Mama! I have always been a picky eater. Nothing ails me!" she answered impatiently, not unlike a wounded animal in a cage, ready to thrash out at anyone who tried to get close.

"If only he'd shown the slightest interest in me, it would not be so intolerable to work side by side with him," she brooded. Sometimes she even hated the coterie of youths who shared Mao's extracurricular activities, especially the three pretty girls from Mao's class who were extremely active in student affairs. She thought they threatened her position. She was jealous of all those who were close to him. She disliked them for taking his attention away from her.

"I need someone to love, to be loved," she thought, "how else could I endure and cope with all these strange new emotions?"

"What's the matter with me, Mama? Everything seems to be so mixed up. I want to do great things, yet I am so self-centered."

"It's part of growing up, daughter," her mother said with understanding, patting her on the shoulders.

Her mother's empathy comforted her. After her forlorn anger, she felt an almost unbearable joy. Hugging her mother, she said, "O Mama, how can you and Papa stand me! I'm so spoiled and willful!"

17

Witness to a Brutal Act

"What do fine horsemen know of aching feet?"
Chinese proverb

WITNESS TO A BRUTAL ACT

Yang K'ai-hui could hardly believe the happiness in which she awoke this morning. She was budding like the lilacs, and seemed to be taking on a sheen like the new grass, a warmth like the spring sun. Although she did not know what the day held, she felt almost breathless with excitement when she opened her eyes and heard the song sparrow singing from the rooftop.

Ignoring the mess in her room, she took time to comb her long shiny hair, all the while admiring her delicately shaped face in the mirror. There were piles of clothes heaped on chairs. The bureau top was cluttered, the floor littered with things dropped and never picked up. The night-stand by her bed was loaded with books and magazines.

"One day if I have the urge," she thought, "I will clean this room with such passionate loathing of untidiness, even a speck of dust on the desk will cause me pain." But this morning she was oblivious of the mess and moved through it without seeing or disturbing it.

Flashing her dimpled smile, she felt content, ready for another day.

Today promised to be like no other day. Mao had asked her to attend and take minutes of the first anniversary special meeting of the New People's Study Society of which he was the director.

The meeting was successful. Thirty students, five female students among them, all enthusiastic and dedicated revolutionaries, had come to reiterate the statement of their goals and a code of by-laws.

> Our aim is to polish our conduct on the
> whetstone of mutual criticism and to pursue
> our studies most earnestly.
> (K'ai-hui had to take down in the minutes,
>   among the club's rules, the following
>   addenda:)
> We will not gamble for money.
> We will not consort with prostitutes.
> We will not fall into slothful idleness.

At the end of the meeting, K'ai-hui suggested that they should incorporate into the statement of their goals, their aim to work for the liberation of women.

She was glad that Mao had immediately rallied to her side. He got up to speak.

"Fellow students, I second Miss Yang's proposal. For no society can claim to be free when half its

176

citizens are dominated and suppressed by the other half."

She was so filled with good feelings again that she wanted to hurry home and tell her mother that she didn't have to wait forever for a man who would accept her as an equal, not a subordinate!

She was deep in thoughts when they came upon crowds of people pouring into the street. There was loud screaming and yelling.

"Punish her, whip her, she's a thief, a thief!"

She saw a big man with bulging muscles pulling a peasant woman. She was stripped half naked. Her nipples were pierced with two wires to which strings were tied. The peasant woman was wailing and pleading. Her tears flowed down her chest, mixed with the blood that flowed profusely from her wounded breasts, dripped onto the road, forming a red path.

"Have mercy my venerable master, I only took a few grains of rice because my baby is starving to death. Have mercy on me!"

But there was to be no mercy. The peasant woman's master landlord, riding in a sedan chair and clad in satin robe and satin shoes, ignored the peasant's plea. He motioned the procession to go on so that all his subjects might see what would happen to them if they were caught stealing from his property.

Mao sprang to his feet, stopped the crowd and calmly reasoned with them.

"Lao chia!" he began. "Before we condemn this woman for stealing, we must first find out why she steals. Like everyone of you, I am sure she works hard in the fields and does her best for her landlord. But less fortunate than you, she did not get enough in return for her labor. She steals because her baby is dying from starvation. There is no other way to save her baby! If your children were starving, wouldn't you do the same?" He paused and the crowd was silent. "Let me ask you another question! Do all of you get fair returns for what you have put in working the fields for this landlord of yours?"

"No," the crowd responded, "We never seem to make enough no matter how hard we toil. He seems to take it all."

Then the wind reversed its direction. The people shouted in unison, "Let the poor woman go! Let her go!"

Like one who had just been resurrected from the dead, the peasant woman prostrated herself in front of Mao, K'ai-hui and all the other students.

"Please not this, woman," Mao said and he knelt down, took his cotton tunic off and draped it over the shoulder of the naked woman.

The miserable lot of the peasant woman shook K'ai-hui to the core.

"It's just awful what we have just seen. Yet hers is not an isolated case, I am sure. How much our people must be suffering, Tse-tung!"

He answered ruefully, "Yes, it is bad. But I have seen worse. Men who had their heads chopped off, their bodies mutilated just because they dared raise their voices against government authority, or dared ask their landlords for a bit more rice. Ours is a very sick society, K'ai-hui!"

His fiery zeal and compassion touched K'ai-hui deeply.

All the more she longed for his affection.

18

Hiding Out

"It is easy to know a man's face, not his heart."
                                        Chinese proverb

"Rich men accumulate money, but poor men accumulate years."
                                        Chinese proverb

HIDING OUT

A year passed quickly. K'ai-hui had worked side by side with Mao in his many extracurricular activities. She helped him distribute thousands of leaflets and pamphlets. She attended countless student organizational meetings with him. She assisted him in putting out the *Hsian River Review*, published by the Hunan Student Union in Changsha, of which Mao was the leader. The publication, edited by Mao in 1919, had gained national recognition among the young intellectuals but had incurred the wrath of Changsha authorities.

By the time of the May Fourth Movement of 1919, Mao began to think of himself as a Marxist.

The May Fourth Movement, in which he participated, was led by students and intellectuals who resented the betrayal of China by the Allied Powers at Versailles. At Versailles, the Allied Powers, except for the United States, had signed secret treaties awarding the Shantung concessions to Japan at the end of World War I.

All Chinese patriots were bitterly disillusioned. This included Mao Tse-tung, who had helped

recruit "coolie armies" for service in Europe during
the war. By exposing the hypocrisy of the Allied
Powers, the May Fourth Movement opened all
China to the inflow of revolutionary ideas which
were further stimulated by the anti-imperialist Russian revolution. At this time Sun Yat-sen turned to
Lenin who quite willingly gave him help.

The May Fourth Movement had important cultural results as well as political consequences. The
written language underwent great changes and
many remaining influences of Confucianism were
rejected.

The patriots had resisted and defeated Japan's
effort to reduce China to a colony through the
"Twenty-one Demands". Students as well as intellectuals were imbued with a great deal of moral and
political conscience. They wanted and agitated for
an end to the warlord rule which had plunged China
into chaotic disunity from 1917-1927.

Together with K'ai-hui, Mao led an unsuccessful
student strike to oust Chang Ching-yao, the tyrannical warlord who controlled Hunan Province mercilessly. The morning after their unsuccessful strike,
Mao came to warn K'ai-hui. "We must leave immediately. The authority has issued warrants for our
arrests. The Siao brothers are waiting for us in
Kiangsi."

It was dark and a grey mist shrouded the lake in

front of her house. Somewhere in the garden a pigeon cooed dolefully, as if to bid a sad farewell. And a dove mourned on, as K'ai-hui turned to look for the second time at the home where she had lived with her family for the past five years.

Mao was disguised as a coolie. He was stripped to the waist and carried big heavy loads. His callous toes stuck out of ragged straw sandals.

"Remember, K'ai-hui," Mao said, "I am supposed to be your porter and you are returning to the country after visiting relatives in Changsha."

They passed all the government check-points without arousing the slightest suspicion. Mao acted coarsely, spitting and swearing petulantly like a true coolie on his job.

Then they came to the last stronghold of the government forces, the last check-point on the outskirts of Changsha near a dense forest. The guard scrutinized their papers for a long time. Then the guard said, "Just one minute! I want you to wait here while I go in my office to do some checking." By this time Mao was convinced the guard had discovered their true identities. He and K'ai-hui abandoned their luggage and ran into the forest.

They hid in the dense bushes of the forest pursued in every direction by government soldiers. Many times the enemy came so close they almost gave up hope and were certain they would be captured. They remained motionless, sometimes not daring to breathe. Dusk came. The soldiers grew weary and the search was called off.

Mao and Yang set off immediately in the direction of Kiangsi, groping and stumbling in the dark. They walked all night without being chased by the enemy until dawn the next day.

They had to escape through obsure paths that were full of pebbles and thorn bushes. Now and then, K'ai-hui stumbled and fell, cutting herself on the knees and legs. She trudged on. Sharp stones had cut through her soft-soled cloth shoes and her feet bled numbly leaving tiny traces of blood upon the thorny paths. Her panting formed clouds of steam in the cold night air. With early dawn came fog and drizzling dew. For miles, the countryside lay in a grey nebulous haze.

"We must push on, for it will soon be light," Mao cautioned. Her steps quickened despite throbbing pain in her feet. "One more hill, K'ai-hui, and beyond that is a friendly little village where we can rest for a few days," Mao tried to cheer her up.

Mustering what little strength she had left, she wobbled onwards.

It was dusk when they arrived at their destination. K'ai-hui felt as if a heavy burden had been lifted from her shoulders but she was so tired that she went to bed without eating, and slept, uninterrupted, until dawn.

186

The next day after a meagre breakfast of rice gruel, Mao helped the farmers in the fields while K'ai-hui stayed behind to help the farmer's wife with domestic chores.

After a long day's work, the peasants again shared their rice gruel, this time with a little more rice grains in it, and salted vegetables.

Though the peasants were very poor, they were happy. They were simple and hard working people and K'ai-hui noticed Mao was very much at home with them.

Mao was smoking and reminiscing with his peasant host. "Has it been almost three years already since my friend Siao Yu and I stopped here on our summer walking tours across Hunan province?" Mao asked.

"Yes, and you were penniless except for a mat and an umbrella you each carried."

"We would have starved to death, Mr. Liu, if it were not for kind people like you who gave us shelter and food."

Mr. Liu smiled with satisfaction and turning around to look at K'ai-hui, he said, "And what a couple of strange youngsters they were!" He chuckled and went on. "Mr. Mao and his friend used to just eat one meal a day at noon time. And each morning they would climb to the top of the hill and remain there for long hours of silent meditation. When they came down, they would swim in the

187

river. One day, we heard shouts in the hill and thought they were being chased by wild animals. We dropped what we were doing and ran to their rescue. But when we got there, we found them inflating their lungs and yelling to the roaring winds. We asked them why they do peculiar things like reciting poetry in the hills and walking until they almost dropped. They told us that they were trying to harden themselves and the shouting and yelling were to train their voices. With all that training I can see why Mr. Mao is in such top physical condition."

"That I am, Mr. Liu!" Mao said jokingly. "In my line of work, life is hectic and dangerous. I must outrun my enemies all the time to avoid capture."

K'ai-hui was glad that in this respect, Mao was in perfect accord with her father who advocated physical training. *"Mens sana in corpore sano.* A sound mind in a sound body," her father would lecture her when she neglected her daily exercise.

Her thoughts flew to her father and she was suddenly seized with pangs of indescribable sadness.

She said good-night and went to sit on her sleeping mat, her knees drawn up and her body hunched over them as though to shelter a deep pain. The fiery energy that had driven her all day seemed to have exhausted itself.

Tears swam in her eyes and streamed from the outer corners down past her cheek bones to her ears. She did not know why she was crying, except that she was frightened and lonely. She nibbled at her sleeves and thought, "Why does Mao still insist on treating me as if I were just another comrade? Why? Even when he is so attentive and concerned about my well being? He is ever so gentle and attentive to my every need! So why?"

Whenever she tried to evaluate her relationship with Mao, there were contradictions that pushed her mind further into chaos. She was awed by his dark inscrutable long face, his high and broad forehead, and his tireless energy. Despite the softening in his large searching eyes and well-formed mouth when he smiled, she had the impression that he was as stubborn as a mule, and that he would wait and watch for years for whatever he set out to obtain but would eventually have his way.

She was especially struck by his perfect blending of a peasant's lively sense of humor with the aloof and introspective qualities of an intellectual. Although he had become a well-known student leader, he still looked and acted like the peasant he was—easy going and simple, qualities that K'ai-hui found most attractive in a man.

Mao and Mr. Liu finally went to bed near midnight.

K'ai-hui could not sleep, so she got up and tiptoed outside, careful not to wake members of the Liu family.

"It's so peaceful outside this time of night!" she muttered to herself as she stood barefoot in the open fields.

The darkness that enveloped the mountain top seemed to watch her every breath. In it was only the gentle stir of the night wind carrying fragrance of honeysuckle and mint. The sky was dark, studded with millions of stars. "How can one sleep on such a beautiful night in the country!" she thought. Then she hummed a little tune and counted the stars. She felt neither sadness nor joy. The stars blinked as though someone in the vast space above was trying to communicate a message of good will. A gentle breeze stirred again and she felt a little chill course through her as she trembled under the immensity of the sky.

Then suddenly, a shuffling of feet punctuated the absolute silence. Somewhere on the slope, a mountain creature was munching on some dry plants. K'ai-hui squinted, and looked all around her. Instead of finding the mountain creature, she saw someone standing at a distance, watching her. She trembled, her face flushed. Even without seeing his face, she knew it was Mao Tse-tung.

She turned her back to him and pretended not to

notice him. She heard his slow steps coming nearer and nearer. She was confused. Her heart pounded. She wanted to stay, yet a small voice inside her told her she should leave. She stood there squirming with indecision, incapable of thinking rationally and unable to walk off and leave him.

He was very close to her now. She could smell the pungent odor of his tobacco. She was seized with a sudden yearning for him. She looked fondly at him in spite of herself. She stared intently on his face which at that instant was tender and full of longing. "Can't you sleep either!" he whispered, "But you might catch a cold standing out here without a coat." He took off his cotton tunic and put it across her shoulders with the sleeves hanging down to her slim waist. Their arms brushed in the mist and K'ai-hui felt a sudden warmth course through her young body.

"You are shivering!" Mao said gently.

She felt weak and tears welled up in her eyes. Before she knew it, she was sobbing and murmuring, "So what if I am, nobody cares anyway!" He wiped her tears away and cupping her hands in his, he said, "You are mistaken, K'ai-hui, I do care." Then he looked away. If only she knew how deeply he cared! There was much he wanted to tell her, but he found himself unable to utter a single word. He would have liked to tell her that he liked the way she

191

walked and held her head, and stuck out her chin as if she didn't have a care in the world. He liked her face because it had a wider range of expression than any face he knew. At one moment she would look happy, relaxed, emotional, passionate. The next moment she would look sad, tense, cold, intellectual. Strong, but malleable, she was self-possessed and strong-willed, she was gentle, yet her gentleness was one she could stiffen if necessary. She looked delicate and fragile, yet underneath the tender frame she possessed a spirit of endurance beyond any he would ever know.

"We must not stay out here too long. There's plenty of work to be done tomorrow," Mao said.

K'ai-hui did not reply but shot a quick glance over his shoulder. Darkness seemed to clutch at their faces again and it was impossible for her to see him clearly. It was as if he had stretched out his hand and caressed her, caressed her to a state of torment and then left her limp and crushed, like a flower trampled on and then discarded among heaps of debris. Love is indeed bitter-sweet, she thought.

She had the eerie yet exhilarating sensation of falling off a cliff, as she descended from the mountain slope with Mao Tse-tung.

19

Return From Exile

"Lights of a thousand stars do not one moon make."
Chinese proverb

RETURN FROM EXILE

By the time Mao and Yang K'ai-hui went back to Changsha from their exile in the countryside, Mao's feeling for Yang contained strata of both affection and respect.

In exile and underground, life was hard. For nearly half a year, she had been running with Mao from village to village. She had endured the dangerous journeys, the uncomfortable lodgings and the scanty meals without complaints. She was like his right-hand man, helping him and goading him on.

Living and working side by side with the peasants had left an indelible mark on her enthusiastic young mind. It had changed her from a self-centered young girl to a matured, caring young woman. Thinking less of herself, she was willing to be integrated into the group of students who dedicated themselves toward reforming and bettering their motherland. She had shown a sense of belonging, of unity and pride. In all her actions, she acted as if she were part of a mystical body, truly possessing *esprit de corps.*

"It's good," Mao thought with satisfaction, "that K'ai-hui has the strength to fight and to withstand the hard life of a true revolutionary! I'll miss her when she leaves for Peking. What if I never see her again!"

The thought put a mysterious tugging in his heart and he felt the premonitory chill of loneliness.

The time between the end of autumn and the beginning of winter was sometimes punctuated with intermittent warm winds and sunshine. Today was such a day, brilliantly clear, the like of which the populace of Changsha had not seen in a long while. The wind was gentle and not a particle of dust stirred. Ideal weather for pleasure-seekers and festivities!

However, there was neither pleasure nor festivity in Mao's heart. The warm sunshine could not lift the fog that shrouded his whole being as he and K'ai-hui stood waiting and gazing down the tracks in the direction from which the train would come. For once he was glad that trains never ran on time.

"I think I hear my train coming now, I can usually hear the whistle from miles away," K'ai-hui said as she lowered her gaze.

People were crowding and pushing to board the train which was noisily starting its engines and clanging its brakes. In the confusion, Mao practically had to shout. "K'ai-hui, will you allow this peasant from Shao Shan to ..." He seemed to be groping for words. But K'ai-hui discreetly began to look away. Mao flushed. It was his habit to stammer

196

whenever he was nervous. She calmly picked up her small bag, and then, as she turned to look at Mao, tactfully finished off his words: "will you write to me, Tse-tung?"

Grasping her hand tightly in his, he seemed reluctant to let her go.

"You must come to Peking soon, Tse-tung!" she told him.

"I will, K'ai-hui, as soon as my work here is finished."

"I probably won't see you for a long time, so do be careful!" she whispered.

Finally, the pain of parting was too great even for him, one with an iron will, who always had strength enough to suppress his desire to speak of what was truly in his heart. He squeezed her hand and said softly and haltingly, "I will miss you, K'ai-hui!" He took her hands and brushed them against his cheeks. At that moment, though every cell in his body pulsated for her, it was the closest he could come to taking her in his arms.

He waved until the train disappeared from sight.

As he left the crowded train station, he felt forlorn. His life had suddenly turned into a desert, immense and empty.

Turning from the present, he abandoned himself to reveries and thought of his mother. "It's unfortunate that Mother never met K'ai-hui. They would have liked each other."

197

20

A Mother's Longing

"Diseases can be cured, fate never."
Chinese proverb

"Life is a dream walking, but death is a going home."
Chinese proverb

A MOTHER'S LONGING

Tse-min, Tse-tan and Tse-hung had been taking turns caring for their mother who had suddenly collapsed one night, and was now bedridden.

Tse-min was boiling the herb medicine that the village doctor had prescribed, while Tse-tan and Tse-hung stood by the bedside of their mother with misty eyes.

"Mama," Tse-min coaxed, "please try a few sips of this. You haven't taken anything for days!"

"But," his mother whispered between gasps, "I do not have enough strength to swallow. Has not Tse-tung come yet?" A sudden look of irreparable sadness filled the otherwise calm face. Dying, she longed to see her first-born whom she loved above all others.

"Tse-tan and Tse-hung are here Mama!" Tse-min said.

"But where is Tse-tung! Does he not want to see me?" She gasped for breath and then continued softly, "Tse-min, can you not go fetch Tse-tung from the temple? I know he is there praying to Buddha. He is the most devout one among you."

She fell into a coma and when she stirred again, she said slowly but clearly, "After I am .gone, will my sons and their father not get along! I particularly worry about Tse-tung."

She blinked back her tears and gazed listlessly at the ceiling. Then, as though she were seeing her oldest son in person and talking to him, her face lighted up and she pleaded, "Would you not take up the beads rather than the sword, Tse-tung? Would you not accept the ways of Buddha? Act by not acting?"

For a jolting second she remembered her husband. "Why is the Severe One not about?"

"He's gone to the city for business, Mama," Tse-min replied, "but he said to show you this letter from Number One Brother. Mama, Number One Brother is coming home to be with you!" Tse-min held up the short note in case his dying mother's eyes should open for a last look upon the world. It was too late. Her eyes remained closed.

In her clouding mind, she had but one thought, her first-born. She made a movement with her hand in front of her and moved her lips. "Tse-tung!"

She convulsed and looked for a moment as if she were better, and then it was all over. Like a lamp before going out, she flared and then gave up her ghost.

Tse-min was glad that his mother's spirit was at least comforted after death.

Her first-born hurried home as soon as he received the bad news. Unfortunately, his mother's hands were already cold when the Number One son entered the gate of the village wall.

21

Mourning for a Gentle Mother

"Peace and tranquility are worth a thousand gold pieces." Chinese proverb

MOURNING FOR A GENTLE MOTHER

Mao Tse-tung had to walk a long distance to his home on his knees, to pay homage to his mother who had died in his absence. He was saddened by her passing. Genuine tears rolled down his expressionless face as he stood by the bier day and night.

The following week Mao Tse-tung, his brothers and sister, were busy making preparations for the funeral feast. They had to give food to all those who came to mourn. They hired professional mourners to wail and mourn at the wake. They invited Buddhist priests to bless the house and to say prayers. They burned paper money and paper boats to insure their mother's journey to her new world.

Everybody mourned. Everybody wore white. But none was more saddened than Mao Tse-tung.

He felt utterly lost and alone in the world, now that his mother was dead. Suddenly she was no more. She would never again put her fragile arms around him to reassure and to comfort him. She would never again say to him, "Be patient! Things will eventually work out for those who suffer in silence."

He looked down at his lifeless mother. Her face

was like a sheet of creased paper, with wrinkles. There were big pouches under her eyes. Her lips were parched and cracked. Her hands were wizened. Her legs were tumid. Her little feet, no more than four inches in length, looked toy-sized in their embroidered shoes.

Poor Mama! He thought angrily of how all her life she had had to carry the whole weight of her body on those little feet! Just because some stupid men thought it beautiful for women to have tiny, deformed feet, half of the Chinese population suffered excruciating pains to have their feet bound and to wobble in mincing steps the rest of their lives. Women have indeed suffered enough! Something should and must be done on their behalf!

Every bone in his body ached with agonizing sadness. The finality of death sent chilling grief through his body and choking grief into his throat. Irreparable sadness pierced his heart like many daggers.

When he was alone by the bier, he touched his mother's hand lightly. It felt icy cold even against his own cold shaking hands.

"Oh kind and gentle Mama! You never did know how much I love and respect you! Why couldn't I bring myself to tell you so? And it's too late now! You'll never know!" he murmured.

Sobbing, he covered his face with his hands. Unable to contain himself any longer, he wept. His heart was frozen with grief.

He remembered a story his mother told him when he was a child.

A young woman gave birth to a baby boy ten years after her marriage. The baby boy grew up to be a handsome, healthy young boy.

One day, while playing among the bushes, the young boy was bitten by a poisonous snake and died. The mother was heart-broken and she went to Buddha to ask him to restore her son to life. Buddha told the sorrowful mother to go and bring him some mustard seeds from the home of people who were not mourning a death. Relentlessly, the mother wandered about, making long journeys in search of such a house.

After many, many years, she was unsuccessful and so she returned to Buddha empty-handed. Upon seeing her again, Buddha said, "When you first came here, you thought you were the only one who had ever suffered a loss through death. Now you know differently. So go in peace, my child! Do not grieve, for the law of death governs us all!"

In the dim candlelight, his mother's oval-shaped face, though wrinkled, seemed alive, untainted, and looked to him at that moment, like a pale magnolia blossom blooming in early spring.

On the way to the cemetery, Mao Tse-tung noticed a pair of pheasants in the field that had been harvested. The beautiful cock pheasant fluttered his wings in an attempt to arouse his more sedately colored hen who lay weakly at his feet. The hen pheasant's right wing was bleeding. She struggled to stand up. But she flopped down again, as if her body was too heavy for her legs. She fluttered her wings a few times and then, exhausted, slumped sideways, dead. The cock pheasant circled around his dead mate a few times as if performing some kind of last rites. Then he walked away, disappearing behind a stack of hay. . . .

Suddenly, a black crow cawed. It descended swiftly and snatched up the dead pheasant. Soaring higher and higher, the crow flew into the clouds. The cock pheasant had lost a mate; the crow gained a meal.

A sudden peace came to the grieving son as he thought: "Thus is the cycle of life! In death one makes room for others. In death one becomes useful to others in the natural order of things and is therefore renewed."

He remembered the peaceful repose of his mother in death. "Only the moment just before the end is a struggle," he thought. "After that, it all seems so restful!"

210

He felt dizzy and weak.

The metal frames on the shining casket glistened in the sun. As they lowered his mother's coffin, he felt as if his whole body were on fire. How he longed to lie down in the cool shade. Numb and sober-faced, he was wrapped up in thoughts of death and was not afraid of it.

How quenching it is for Mother to be lying seven feet under in the cool, cool earth!

22

Encounter With a Brother

"Brothers are like hands and feet." Chinese proverb

ENCOUNTER WITH A BROTHER

When the funeral ceremony was over, Mao immediately started to pack his belongings which consisted mainly of books.

He was startled when Tse-min came in quietly behind him. *"Ta Ko*[1], are you leaving already?" Tse-min asked. "I was hoping you would stay a little longer this time."

"I am sorry to leave so soon, Tse-min. Now that Mother is gone there's no reason for me to stay any longer or to ever come back again! But I'll try to find a way to get you, Tse-tan and Tse-hung, out of this place after I have a job."

"Yes, and you only have N years to go before you land one!" Tse-min said sarcastically.

Tse-tung had spoken quietly, yet Tse-min understood the weight of his oldest brother's words. The one moment Tse-min most dreaded had come. His oldest brother had finally said he was going away and was never coming back!

Tse-tung's decision struck his younger brother like a typhoon sweeping across the plains, taking

[1]Number One Older brother

and destroying everything in sight, razing it to the ground.

Tse-min was in despair. Although the habit of admiring his oldest brother was too strong to be overcome easily, it was not impossible for him to feel, momentarily, a sense of betrayal. All these years his oldest brother had shirked his responsibility as the Number One son of the family. Since the age of fourteen, Tse-min had to shoulder all the responsibilities vacated by his oldest brother who was the rightful heir apparent of the family. All during Tse-min's adult years, he had to stay behind to help his father with the farms.

"How could Oldest Brother be so thoughtless and heartless as to leave all the responsibilities to me," Tse-min thought silently. "He knows very well that I don't get along with Father either. He must realize I, too, would want to leave home to go out and see the world. He must know it's impossible for me to do so unless he shares some of the family obligations. Tse-tan and Tse-hung are still too young to take over. How can he possibly not see my point of view? It is out of character for Oldest Brother to be inconsiderate and, more so, to be without compassion. So why? So why?"

Tse-min reached this juncture of his secret thoughts and gave himself an answer: "It's fate!

Nothing more! Just like Mama used to remind me when she was alive."

The memory of his gentle mother, though painful for Tse-min, had a strange, cheery effect on him. He was suddenly able to accept his destiny with resignation, and without resentment toward his oldest brother.

He sighed loudly, gave a slight shrug and said, "Well, *Ta Ko,* I guess I'll just have to get used to the fact that you are not coming home anymore. I was predestined to live out my life with our ill-tempered father!" Tse-min swallowed hard and then resumed, "But I guess it's just as hard for him to have to contend with us, too! You, for one, *Ta Ko,* drive Papa up the wall with your disregard for material possessions, and your talk about equal distribution of land."

"Do I really bother Papa that much?" Tse-tung asked in jest.

"You are no apple of his eyes, *Ta Ko,* that's for sure!"

"More like a big grain of sand swimming in them, eh?"

Gesturing and laughing, Tse-min added, "And a feather forever tickling his nose!"

"No wonder he sneezes everytime I come near him!"

"Papa is especially allergic to your modern ideas! He says you harbor too much of that modern junk in your head!"

The two brothers laughed with the abandonment of children at play, though they were both in their mid-twenties.

Tse-min was the first to stop laughing and said seriously, "I hear you are quite taken by Yang K'ai-hui. She must be very special!"

At the mention of Yang, Tse-tung's face lighted up and there was longing in his eyes as he said, "Yes, Tse-min, *that* she is!"

"*Ta Ko,* are you getting married soon? You haven't forgotten you are going to be twenty-six in a few months!"

"Don't worry Tse-min! I will, someday, when I am ready!" Tse-tung's mouth twitched slightly with embarrassment and tersely dismissed the subject of love and marriage.

"Are you returning to Changsha, *Ta Ko?*"

"Yes, but not for very long. I am going to Peking shortly."

23

Reunion of Young Lovers

"Happy people do not count hours as they pass."
                                        Chinese proverb

REUNION OF YOUNG LOVERS

Changsha was reeking with heat when Mao arrived. But he ignored the scorching heat of summer and joined with two thousand factory workers for a sit-in strike.

Sweat bathed his body. The factory was hot and humid. Outside, the sun glared through layers of dust, streaked by skies of black soot. Gusts of hot wind blasted his face, bringing with it the stench of urine and decayed garbage. The heat became more oppressive by late afternoon, and it hung around his neck like soggy gunnysacks.

Mao wrote K'ai-hui as soon as the strike was over. "... Though our demands for equal pay and better working conditions were not met, we have nevertheless made a beginning. Even if the protest did not yield successful results, the ideas behind it will survive."

So summer slid easily into fall.

As Mao walked across the campus amidst the flaming beauty of an autumn afternoon, when the sun shone on and brought out the deepest shades in the red and orange leaves of the maples and the

221

birches, he was carried away by shouts of his student followers. "Down with all warlords in China!"

Inspired by Mao's public lecture introducing Marxism, the students cried, "Marxism for China!"

Mao was careful not to stay long. By now, he had become the acknowledged leader of the radicals and had thousands of student followers in Hunan. The authority followed his every move. With a concomitant increase in civil strife, banditry, anarchy and widespread corruption in every province of China, every rebel's life was in danger.

As Mao hurried away from the crowd, he seemed to see Yang K'ai-hui's dimpled smile everywhere.

A twinge of desire stirred within him. The pulsation in his body, and the pulsation of the city, seemed to be slowly sinking in unison, languidly and more languidly with the setting sun. How he longed to be with her!

When he was safe in his apartment, Mao put finishing touches on the poems that he had written for K'ai-hui.

They were tender, touching utterings of love, pain, sorrow, duty and even murmurs of unrequited passion.

While the city spent the night in wakefulness, Mao sat in his bare room, listening to the last of the summer mosquitos hum against the cotton netting he had tacked in his window. Parting the curtains, he peered fearfully down the street for signs of danger. As he drank his tea nervously, he thought of what to do if the war lord Ho Chien's soldiers came.

When the danger had passed, he immediately began on a new poem. As he wrote, his thoughts drifted toward Peking and K'ai-hui. How intricate are my feelings for her!

Thinking of her he suddenly remembered an ancient ballad he had known as a young boy:

> In a boundless night
> Darkness enshrouds the human heart
> Only the fires of earthly passion
> Blaze and die with life.

In his loneliness and solitude, he wrote poetry which spurred him on and cushioned his falls into depression. The poems, like manna from heaven, gave food for his starving soul. As though receiving a blood transfusion, his emaciated spirit was revived and soared again to a new high and he enthusiastically counted off the days until the first of winter.

"Only three more months and I'll be there!" he muttered.

When from the North came the first gusty flurries of yellow dust, Mao breathlessly prepared for his journey to Peking.

The last two days seemed the longest. He could neither eat nor sleep.

But at the last minute, Mao had to change his plans. The atmosphere in Changsha was so charged with revolutionary ardor that he felt it his duty to stay on and channel the students' reformist enthusiasm into his camp. He lived only for the revolution and he propagandized his beliefs spontaneously and continuously. Despite his preoccupation with revolutionary activities, he was lonely.

Spring came. By then Mao was confident some of the student leaders were able to carry on his work in Changsha. So he booked for passage on the train with the last of his savings, and left Changsha for Peking.

It was crowded and suffocating in the train. The seats were hard and uncomfortable. But the countryside was breathtaking, ineffably beautiful and peaceful under an azure sky. Flowers were blooming, trees were green with new leaves. Farmers were busy plowing their fields. Roads, bridges, swollen streams and brooks occasionally appeared. Young girls, dressed in light summer frocks, crowded the banks of streams and brooks washing loadfuls of clothing. Their faces, expressionless were reflected in the water. There was no chatter or laughter save the sound of clothes beating against the rocks. For miles this pastoral scene, in all its simplicity, unrolled like a scroll before him.

He wondered how many of those farmers he had seen actually tilled their own land. How many of those young girls washing clothes were servants, sold by their parents to houses of the rich in years of famine? Like slaves, they lived in captivity. Some of them might be resold, beaten or raped.

He thought of the elites, the fifteen percent of the rich and the powerful in the country, who lived off the fat of the land, and who were content. Theirs was a life of plenty: plenty of food, plenty of children, plenty of wives and concubines, plenty of culture and art, plenty of time to engage in self-gratification.

He thought of his comrades, mostly young men and women, who saw the injustice and inequality of the system and who were willing to risk their lives to change it. But men with power and guns were always there, ever ready to jail or cut them down.

"How can we ever hope to succeed," he thought. "We are but a few. But we must have conviction, persistence and faith. For these three things working hand in hand, can move mountains."

Their problems were indeed mountainous.

Since the founding of the Republic on October 10, 1911, there was not one government strong enough to unite the country. Sun Yat-sen, who became President of the Republic after Hsuan Tung, the young Emperor of the Ching Dynasty, abdicated in 1912, and was forced, a few days later, to resign the presidency in favor of Yuan Shih-kai. Yuan proclaimed himself Emperor of the Great Constitutional Dynasty in 1915, but died a year later.

After the death of Yuan Shih-kai, the capital of Peking, recognized by the foreign powers as the seat of the legitimate government, became a shuttlecock, tossed back and forth between contending warlords who were primarily interested in self-aggrandizement.

"It's three years now since Yuan's death and Sun Yat-sen and his followers are still in exile, unable to establish a stable government," Mao thought in despair. "China is like a plate of fine, dry sand, so easily divided and scattered!"

Chinese could not communicate with each other easily for there are hundreds of dialects spoken all through China. The only effective means of communication was the written language. But the majority of the population could not read.

Most Chinese were cliquish and clannish, reluctant to accept outsiders from other villages and provinces.

Mao was afraid he would not be accepted in Peking. The garlic-eating northerners had always regarded southerners as shifty, quick-tempered, crude, unreliable revolutionaries.

In a lighter mood now, Mao thought that he would miss the small red peppers of Changsha valley, where clusters of the hot condiment were grown in every free space.

At this juncture, he opened a tiny crack in the window, and streams of cold air, seeping through, blew gently on his face, reminding him of his mother's caress when he was little. In contrast to the memory of his gentle mother, he could almost hear the angry cry of his father, "Why, what have I done, that heaven inflicts upon me such a son! He is unfilial, fiery and stubborn as a mule!"

Mao chuckled to himself. Me, a mule! Well, better to be thought of as a mule than a turtle egg!

As the train sped northward, the advance spring of the south became ´tentative. The terrain changed abruptly. The gentle rolling hills gave way to high jagged mountains; the fecund lush green to sterile barren brown. Trees were leafless; withered, brittle branches hung on them precariously. Now and then, there were weak assertions of growth. In the gaunt scene, wild, miniature bushes were blooming in torrents of pale flowers. These flowers were of such pale hues, that though in abundance they lay inconspicuously in a desolate land still blighted and ravaged by the late exit of winter.

"Though we are many now," Mao thought, "our voices, like the pale hue of those wild flowers, are still too weak and too disorganized to be heard above the roarings of the ruling few."

Staring at the precipitous mountains under lowering clouds, he felt dwarfed and reduced to insignificance. He marvelled at the vastness and magnificence of China. Yet he was saddened by the fact that only ten percent of this majestic land was arable. Millions still toiling in extreme poverty!

Someone would rise up to lead these poverty-stricken people. Someone would put everything right and would again waken the sleeping giant that was China and would lead her out of humiliation to victory. "We will," he vowed, "my comrades and I will loosen the claws of repression! So brave and courageous, my comrades! So full of new ideas, but still so destitute of popular support!"

His mood oscillated. He felt defeated and insignificant; his goals unreachable. But suddenly light-hearted, he realized that he had hardly believed he was actually on his way to Peking, the city of a thousand traditions. Not yet there, he yearned to see its ancient wonders.

He finally arrived, several hours ahead of schedule, penniless, but in high spirit.

Peking was still in the grip of winter. The dry winter monsoon was blowing from the Gobi desert, stirring up clouds of dust, blinding him and striking his face like pins.

"Aiya! It's too cold here for comfort, K'ai-hui! But it's good to see you!" He looked fondly at her.

"Now my heart is no longer empty!" K'ai-hui thought and blinked back tears of joy.

After the initial excitement of seeing K'ai-hui again, Mao reverted to his calm ways.

"For the first few days I'll have to impose on your family, K'ai-hui. Your gateman has already agreed to let me share his *k'ang*[1] till I find some place to live."

"Yes, Tse-tung, I have already talked to Papa about it," K'ai-hui said.

She's the same little dynamite who sees to my every need, Mao thought gratefully. He was speechless with happiness. He wanted to lay bare before her all the longings he endured during their long separation, but he was too shy. Finally he said in a tight voice, "Thank you K'ai-hui!"

For days they walked around in a daze, floating carelessly from one thing to another. They read the Communist Manifesto, Kautsky's Class Struggle and Kirkupp's History of Socialism.

They were happy!

---

[1] A brick bed, heated from below, that is warm in winter but cool in summer.

24

Lodging at the "Three Eyes Well"

"A toad would be silly to plan a meal of goose!"
Chinese proverb

LODGING AT THE "THREE EYES WELL"

After a week of searching, Mao came in one morning and announced excitedly, "K'ai-hui, I won't have to impose on your family any longer! I've found a place which I'll share with seven other Hunanese friends."

"Is it far from here?" K'ai-hui asked.

"No. It's quite close to here and within walking distance to the University of Peking. Incidentally, this little two-room house is called 'Three Eyes Well'!"

"What a name!" K'ai-hui said. They both laughed.

"Are the two rooms big? And do you plan to have four to a room?" K'ai-hui inquired.

"No, the rooms are very small. And we plan to have eight in a room. The second room does not have a *k'ang*. We'll use it as the study."

"You mean all eight of you packed fast on one *k'ang*, Tse-tung! Heaven forbid! You won't have room even to breathe!"

"In my condition, K'ai-hui, one can't afford to think of breathing!" Mao laughed and continued. "At any rate, all eight of us promise to be careful.

233

Whenever one of us wants to turn over, he has to warn people on each side of him!"

"What if all eight of you decide to turn at once?"

"Then we'll have to take turns just as we have to take turns with this coat we bought to share among us."

"Are all eight of you the same size?"

"Far from it. I am the tallest and we range from 5'3" to 6'2"."

"How do you buy one coat to fit everybody?"

"No problem! We just added our height and averaged from that." They both laughed again. Mao said, "I hope none of them snores!"

"And how about lice?" K'ai-hui said mischievously.

In a more serious mood, K'ai-hui inquired, "How's the first day of work in the library?"

"Fine, not too busy. Mr. Li Ta-chao, the University Librarian, is a very good man to work for."

"Yes," K'ai-hui said, "from what I heard, he is very understanding and kind and always willing to lend a sympathetic ear."

"He is urging me to join the Young China Association. Do you know anything about this association, K'ai-hui?"

Nodding her head, she said, "It's dedicated to mobilize patriotic opposition to any pro-Japanese government." She paused and brushing her hair from her face, she continued, "You should meet a great many well-known people coming to the library."

"Today Hu Shih came but he was too busy to talk to me. I am only an assistant librarian. I check out books for them and see to it the library is kept clean and the books tidy!"

Despite his miserable living conditions, despite the shabbiness of his only gown, despite the clerical position he held in the library, despite his "lowly" southern accent, Mao was happy in Peking.

He was happy to be near K'ai-hui, his first love. To him, she was the breath of spring, evergrowing and hopeful amidst the blight of winter.

For Mao and Yang, Peking was suddenly enchanting, a winter wonderland. Together they walked through parks and the old palace grounds. They touched and admired the multitudes of trees lining the sidewalks. They saw the white plum blossoms flower while the ice still held solid over *Pei Hai.* Ice crystals, sparkling like diamonds and gems, hung from willows that stood along the banks of the lake.

"They are absolutely magnificent, K'ai-hui! These must have inspired the *T'ang* poet, Tsen Tsan to write about *Pei Hai's* winter-jewelled trees, looking like ten thousand pear trees blossoming."

The flames in his heart burning for her melted the snow of loneliness of a provincial traveler longing for his home. And together they waited and hoped for an early spring.

25

Young Lovers in Peking

"Heaven is only three feet above one's head."

Chinese proverb

YOUNG LOVERS IN PEKING

Spring came, neither early nor late.

Mao was so much in love, time seemed to flow swiftly by, like water running down stream, slipping through his finger tips, irretrievable. And before he knew it, it was autumn, the season of colorful leaves and chrysanthemums. Dreamily, he held K'ai-hui's hand and together they watched the glassy yellow bricks of the palaces and the pagodas on the hills.

Floating in a small boat, they scrutinized and were transfixed by the flame-like maples around the lake. The water rippled, and the reflection of the numerous maple trees danced and swayed under them.

"Heavenly!" he exclaimed, and nestled close to her, almost capsizing the boat. And there he lay, his head buried in her bosom. He heard the fierce beating of her heart.

"Let's stay to watch the sunset!" he suggested.

It was an idyllic time to stroll along the lake which by now was deserted. Except for the litter of the day, cigarette butts, bits of paper and other assortments of trash, the park was empty. For miles, not a living thing could be seen. Silence and peacefulness pervaded here that just a few hours ago was teeming with people who had crowded the whole area with their picnic lunches, breaking the tranquility with their boisterous laughter.

Mao and K'ai-hui walked leisurely along the lake, the sand tickling their bare feet. They were both silent. But in silence or speech, the communication between them never stopped. Their hearts beat in unison to the rhythm of the waves.

From time to time they stopped to throw pebbles in the water. The swishing sound that the pebbles made when they hit the water mingled strangely with the sound of the wind whistling through the branches of the ancient trees. Happiness coursed through Mao's young body as he watched K'ai-hui slice pebbles over the water surface gracefully, and with scientific precision. Never before had he felt so intensely: the caress of the wind, the freshness of the lake water, the fragrance of the afternoon air. The wind sang a song that, instead of bringing autumn chill, spiked and intoxicated the twilight with love and romance. It was as if the wind blew away all the loneliness gathered within him since morning, when he decided to leave Peking and accept a job in Changsha. Sitting so close to K'ai-hui, his shoulder almost touching hers, he contemplated life with romantic fancy, preoccupied neither with the past nor the future. He closed his eyes and dozed off.

When he woke up, K'ai-hui was sitting opposite him with her knees drawn up and her chin above them.

"How young and beautiful she looks! And how I wish she were going back to Changsha with me!" Mao thought. He felt a heaviness weighing him down. It was as if someone had stolen his happiness away while he slept.

"Why did I keep my plans secret? Why couldn't I bring myself to ask her?" he asked himself angrily.

"Did you have a nice nap?" K'ai-hui said as she slid down beside him. "K'ai-hui," Mao hesitated, "I've been wanting to tell you—I am leaving Peking in two weeks. Professor Yi P'ei-chi of Changsha Normal College—you remember him—is now head of the school and he asked me to teach Chinese literature at the college and to head the primary school attached to the Normal College."

"How long have you known about this offer of jobs, Tse-tung?"

"Since this morning."

"And you kept it a secret for a whole day!"

"Well," Mao paused, "well, I have something I want to talk to you about but I couldn't seem to muster enough courage until now."

There was another long pause then Mao said awkwardly, "K'ai-hui, will you go back to Changsha with me? Now that I have a job, we can be married as soon as I find a place for us to live."

241

K'ai-hui was stunned—but happy. Despite her feminist views, she showed the traditional dependence of the well-bred Chinese lady.

"Of course Tse-tung, I mean yes, but we must first ask my parents' permission."

The earth whirled underneath her feet and she whispered silently in her heart: "A poet! A principal! A lecturer! A true revolutionary! A champion of women's rights! And loving me! Surely I must be the luckiest woman alive!"

Mao reached for her hand. Above the lake, a deep blue sky, tipped with orange, stretched to the western horizon. The lake flowed into the orange and the colors blended where they met. Gradually, the blue grew darker; it turned almost purple. For a split second, the orange turned to a blaze of light yellow. It grew stronger and stronger. Then almost immediately, the radiance flashed and dimmed. After giving its last glow, the sun slipped over the edge of the earth. With its dying light it steeped the shimmering lake in silvery grey.

They stood looking at the lake, in deep thought. They were happy. But their eyes did not meet and their thoughts stayed separate and fell into the water and were carried out to the open sea.

26

Nuptials

"While friendships last as long as meat and wine,
marriages last as long as rice and fuel."
Chinese proverb

NUPTIALS

The late September sun in Changsha shone more intensely even than at the height of summer. But all too quickly, sunset came so early it was startling, and the long nights deepened quickly into silence.

Morning, noon and night, the sky was always full of clouds, moving and covering the whole sky except for a few rifts of dark blue.

On the eve of K'ai-hui's wedding day, the weather turned oppressively humid, and a greasy clamminess clung to her skin. Suddenly, a wind of uncertain strength and direction sprung up and rain fell intermittently, stopping only to start again.

There was in this wind and rain a special mysterious power which transmitted a music to K'ai-hui's young heart, a music never heard in spring or summer. She heard temple bells at eight this evening, which in summer often could not be heard for the clatter of people strolling in the evening cool, now brought a midnight hush to the vicinity. Crickets chirped loudly. The lamplight took on an unusual brightness. Autumn. And K'ai-hui, for the first time, felt that autumn was not as hateful as people said, that it really was not a time of anticipated loneliness.

It should be cool after the rain, K'ai-hui thought joyfully, as she curled her lovely long hair with a pair of hot iron tongs. It will be a good day tomorrow for me to marry.

There were so many last minute details to attend to for the wedding ceremony that September day in 1920, that K'ai-hui did not have time to dwell and savor the true meaning of this auspicious occasion, this day of days, until late in the night, when the last guest departed.

Despite her feminist views, and her revolutionary zeal, she regarded her marriage with a great deal more reverence than many non-radical women. No doubt K'ai-hui thought that she opposed the bourgeois concept of marriage, but she never approved of any alternative to monogamy. Even though she was opposed to polygamy, she did not condemn the current trend, popular among young radicals, in advocating 'free love'!

It was just a simple wedding with only a few relatives and close friends. Well wishers were in and out, congratulating the newlyweds all day long. It was well into the night when Mao and Yang were at last alone together in their bridal chamber.

Yang heard his massive movements and his slow steps. In he came, handsome in his new night gown. His face was bright with desire, his bearing a triumph. Hastily, he took away his gown. For the first time Yang saw him naked, splendid in his young manhood. She flung the bed cover away and pulled him down to her. In the mysterious darkness, they embraced, kissed and whispered endearments in each other's ears, while their hearts beat in unison to the rhythm of the night.

"I wish this moment would never end, Tse-tung!" To which he responded with more kisses, first yearningly, then passionately, and finally with desires of such intensity that they soon were locked in ecstasy, oblivious to the troubles that were brewing throughout China.

The ground seemed to open up and totally engulf her as he entered her. Ying and yang united! Every cell in her body came alive and beat with such force that she swayed and responded to him, until in unison their passions were spent. He had inspired her to ecstasy! She caressed his limp, relaxed body and rolling over, kissed the mole on his chin.

The next morning, she was awakened by the rustling of leaves outside her window. She glanced out. A pearl grey shadow was just twining itself around the boughs of the willow tree along the east side of the lake. Since the rest was still in darkness, she lingered under the quilt, so cozy and warm. She was happy. But her happiness was marred and her spirit dampened when she thought of her father's sudden death four weeks ago. Though Mao did not break down as she did, she knew he, too, was deeply affected by the untimely death of her father. "I've lost a great teacher!" he had said sadly.

K'ai-hui remembered how excited her father was when he heard Mao and she were to be married.

"I am pleased! I am indeed pleased! You deserve the best, daughter. And he is the best!"

For days, he was like a little boy, shuttling from shop to shop looking for a nuptial gift for his daughter. Finally he told K'ai-hui excitedly, "I've found the perfect bed for you. And what's more, the salesman has given me another smaller bed at half price. You can keep the smaller one in the guest room for me when I come to visit!"

She had wanted to postpone the wedding, but her mother urged her to go ahead with the plan. "Papa would want it this way," her mother said. "It was his axiom to concentrate on the living and not mourn senselessly for the dead."

K'ai-hui felt her throat tightening as she ran her fingers along the silk cloth on the lattices which were supported by the bed posts. How well Papa knew my taste! Such beautiful paintings of birds and flowers. And how well this pink bedspread brings out the intricate grains of the rosewood bed frames.

"A bit too big and too pretentious for two hot-blooded revolutionaries like us, K'ai-hui!" Mao had said upon seeing the bed that occupied close to half of the entire floor space. "But I like it!" he quickly added.

To take her mind off sad thoughts, K'ai-hui began to plan in her mind how she would decorate her new home. And what a lovely home for a newlywed couple! It was located in beautiful surroundings in the outskirts of Changsha. The area was quiet and had a beautiful lake and a garden full of flowers and trees.

"In the spring I'll plant more flowers and trees in the garden!" K'ai-hui told her husband.

In the house, she would put a little door mat at the entrance on the right side of the building and maybe a large mat on the dirt floor of the room adjacent to it. This room would be the guest room. The room on the right side of the dirt-floored room she would make into a study for her husband. In it she would put all the furniture they owned, a big table, a chair, and a lamp. In the room on the left of the study, she would put a big wooden box and cover it with a table cloth for a dining table, and two small wooden boxes for chairs.

"There would be nothing left for the bed room!" she said sadly to her husband.

"The bed is decorative enough without more furniture in the room!" her husband consoled her.

"If we can afford a little extra, and if I am not too busy, I might even make curtains for all the windows Tse-tung!"

249

"I didn't know you had such good house-keeping skills, my little Poplar!" Mao teased her. "Truly the mistress of No. 22, Ching Hui Tang, Changsha City, Hunan!"

"How did you come upon such a lovely house, Tse-tung? I just love it! Even the name of the street, *Ching Hui Tang* has a musical ring to it. Do you think we'll stay here for a long time?"

But she never did have the extra she hoped for nor did she have the time to do anything beyond the minimum in the house. As soon as their two-day honeymoon was over, her home became the center for underground activities in Changsha and the adjacent areas. By this time Mao had become the acknowledged leader among revolutionaries in Hunan.

Beside helping her husband conduct the multifarious underground activities at home, K'ai-hui attended all the political rallies he organized. She was always there, urging him on behind the scene. Never once did she want the spotlight on herself. Helping him in his revolutionary work had become the *summum bonum* of her life. She found fulfilment in serving him. Her love for him had mingled with her firm devotion to the ideal of revolution.

"I am proud of you, Tse-tung!" she said. "You are now a political evangelist! Wherever you go, there are converts!"

Many years in advance of the rest of China, Yang had founded her private cult of Mao who was for her the embodiment of the revolution of her idealistic dreams. Mao's love for her and hers for him was the emotional basis of their first year of marriage.

Mao was the center and pivot of her life. For him, she gave up hours of sleep in order to participate in all his deep-into-the-night political discussions. For him, she copied laboriously by hand, all the minutes of such important meetings, because by now, a year after their marriage, they had both become members of the Communist Party. She was a devoted wife, slavishly indulgent as far as her husband's physical comforts were concerned. She gave him the choicest cuts of meat, the freshest, greenest vegetables and the juiciest fruits. And he was a most gentle, loving husband, attentive to her every need.

"My precious Poplar, you must stay home to rest this time," Mao told her.

"But I do want to attend the first meeting of the Party! And Tse-tung, I've never been to Shanghai!" she argued.

Mao would not acquiesce. "You must rest and try to recover from your cold! We can't go to any of those nice Shanghai Parks anyway! The foreigners have signs that say 'Chinese and Dogs not allowed' all over the place!"

K'ai-hui knew her husband was often pained by

such humiliation forced on their country by foreigners. Like a ripe watermelon, China was easily carved into pieces by invaders with superior arms. Dared she hope that one day, her husband, together with all those working for the good of her people would rectify all that?

"But I'll miss you, K'ai-hui!" Mao said.

He had never ceased to wonder how desirable she was. It was hard for him to be near her and not make love to her.

"I want so much to have you near me wherever I go, K'ai-hui!" Tenderly he fondled and roused her, then, direct as he always was, took her, penetrating into the kernel of her being as if to drain all his love and anguish into her. His intensity hurt her a little. But already climaxed, she cried out in pleasure.

She felt great satisfaction that he loved her with such intense desire and passion. She was all woman and returned his passion with more passion. She thought him all man, with greatness above most men.

She knew with pride that he regarded her not only as his wife and his only love, but as his companion and friend, compatible in all matters that were important to him.

She cherished with much pride too, the numerous, most intimate poems he had written for her. In them, he had eulogized her not only as his beautiful wife, but as a clever and witty lover as well.

"Let's be lovers, forever! Tse-tung!" She was not without shame and guilt when she afforded herself to thoughts of her passion and her burning desire for her husband's body. But most of the time she thought of the revolution and wondered what the future would really be if their ideology, Communism, were to triumph in China. Between these thoughts which were in her mind every day, there ran weaving and interweaving the thought of possible danger and separation.

Convinced that if the revolution were to be successful there would be violence, bloodshed and even death, she tried to prepare herself for any eventuality. Yet she was afraid, and thought it unbearable if anything should happen to her husband.

"Aiya! The pain would be too great for me! Do be careful Tse-tung! Do not take unnecessary risks, for soon there will be three of us!"

And so Mao left for Shanghai to attend the First Congress of the Chinese Communist Party at the end of June, 1921.

27

Fruit of a Happy Union

'Blessings never come in pairs, ills never alone."
Chinese proverb

"There has never been a birth without the collaboration of Heaven."
Chinese proverb

FRUIT OF A HAPPY UNION

Their son, An-ying was born two years after they were married.

"My happiness is now complete!" K'ai-hui thought with maternal pride, as she nursed and watched her first born grow.

Mao's happiness was further enhanced by success in his revolutionary work. With the help of Li Li-san, a Moscow-trained revolutionary, he set up schools for the Anyuan miners. He became Chairman of the Association of Hunan Trade Unions.

Unfortunately, his notoriety incurred displeasure and wrath from the provincial government.

The Maos' newly found stability and happiness ended one night when Li Shao-chi, a comrade from Ninghsiang, a village twenty-four miles from Mao's village of Shao Shan, came to warn them. "Comrades, you must leave immediately. The authority has issued warrants for your arrest."

Leaving most of their possessions behind, the Maos went underground. K'ai-hui, carrying An-ying papoose-style, trudged on.

An-ying stirred. He whined for food. Such sounds that normally were sounds of joy in the Mao household, became threats to their safety. Still, there was no time to stop.

"We must push on before they overtake us!" Mao cautioned.

K'ai-hui pressed her son's little hand to her cheeks. "My precious, my dear little An-ying!" She was glad that he was still too young to have any knowledge of the pain, suffering, hatred and violence that were seething everywhere around them. Although An-ying was heavy on her back, she was comforted by the warmth of his little body, so close she could hear his little heart beating.

"We must struggle on. For An-ying and millions like him. For their children and their children's children." Thinking thus, her steps quickened despite throbbing pain in her feet.

For the next three years, she and An-ying went with Mao everywhere whenever possible. As long as she was with him, she did not mind the tedious and sometimes dangerous journeys, the uncomfortable lodgings and the scanty meals.

Life had been so fulfilling with her husband and child that K'ai-hui had not thought of her father for a long time. When she was a little girl, her father was her love, her mentor, her pillar of strength. Since her marriage, her husband had become all that, and more. She could not imagine life without him!

The revolution marched on. Mao had gradually emerged into national prominence. Still he kept on defying the Comintern's policy and instead, concentrated on works in agrarian revolt.

He repeatedly repudiated the edict of the Moscow-trained faction in the Chinese Communist Party that the peasants might assist but not play a primary revolutionary role.

"But comrades," Mao persisted, even though his proposal was rejected by the Comintern, "peasants form 85% of our population!"

Since he had advanced to the Chairmanship of All China's Peasants' Union, he was often away, visiting other provinces. These trips were hectic and dangerous. K'ai-hui, unable to accompany him because of their young child, could only sit and wait for his return with a heavy heart.

She loved him and admired him more and more. The few times they were together, she treasured each moment as though it were the last.

And she stirred him still. The combination of her fine, oval-shaped face, her tiny mouth, her smallness, her fragile look, her supple body set his heart throbbing and desire gripped him with such force that at times it became uncontrollable. When he embraced her, she was so delicate he felt as if she would break. Yet she was strong and malleable.

"It's good, my Poplar, that you have the strength to fight, to endure the hard life of a true revolutionary!" Mao had often said to her.

She loved his simplicity and his naturalness of a Chinese peasant. She understood his lively sense of humor and she never tired of hearing his rustic laughter.

"As long as I can hear your jolly laughter I fear nothing, Tse-tung!"

"Oh my dear dear K'ai-hui! How I wish I didn't have to leave again! But I must, tomorrow. The Nationalists have declared the Communist Party illegal, and have given orders to arrest all Party members. The new governor of Hunan, Ho Chien, has placed a price of five hundred yuan on my head.

"You and An-ying are to stay with my sister Tse-hung, in the country until I send for you. Since I can't get support from Li Li-san who echoes the view of Moscow, I've organized a small band of remnants and volunteers called the First Regiment of the First Division of the First Workers and Peasants Revolutionary Army. We'll retreat to Chingkangshan, the Well Ridge Mountain, on the Hunan-Kiangsi border. It's a remote district, difficult of access where forests and terrain would dilute the police power of the provincial authorities."

That night he took her grimly, yet ever so lovingly, as though he wanted to seal her to him forever so that no physical separation could ever take her away from him.

K'ai-hui felt dizzy from feelings of simultaneous grief and satisfaction, until all realities ceased to exist and she was in a deep, dark, selfish world where only togetherness with her husband mattered. For a brief moment, veiled by sadness, she wondered what she wanted most, a father for her children, or victory of their cause for the Chinese people.

28

Separation

"Two barrels of tears do not heal a wound."
                                    Chinese proverb

SEPARATION

Separated from her husband, and sick from her second pregnancy in six years, K'ai-hui had to force herself to go on, day after day, with her usual routine of caring for An-ying while she waited for words from Juichin, a small jute and hemp center in southeastern Kiangsi, where Mao and his comrades had built the Central Soviet Base.

In exile and underground, life was lonely, hard. But at least she and An-ying were safe. She waited. Still no word. And she thought the lonely months would never end.

The child grew heavy within her. She was small and carried it with much difficulty. But she was proud of it. The little movements inside her reminded her of her husband's love. An-ying, their first born, now five years old, was a source of joy for her.

"Part of you, my dear husband, stays with me in our son, and another one formed from our love will soon be born."

After nearly eight months, she was glad that she could at least send this brief message to her husband through a member of the underground. Her husband, however, could not write to her.

She longed to be at his side, to counsel him whenever she could, to warn him against his enemies, to remind him that he must take care of himself. She suddenly felt sorry for him, because he was so strong yet so weak, so organized yet so disorganized. In mid-winter, he would often go coatless unless she reminded him. His obstinacy was so great that it might cause him to fall.

"He is marked for success, yet true happiness I doubt he will ever know. Who, beside myself, truly loves him?" K'ai-hui thought, and was desolate for him.

Absence deprived her of his physical presence but never of his spiritual closeness, or the many memories they had shared. His gaiety lingered on in her dreams, giving her strength in time of tribulation. She saw his kind face in the face of An-ying and heard his hearty laugh in the life-beat of their infant yet unborn. She remembered his tenderness when, between Party work, they lay on a plot of grass under beautiful trees on many idle Sunday afternoons in Peking's Western Hills.

"You are so distracting, K'ai-hui! But I love you!" Those words sang in her heart again and again.

Month passed into month. And still no news from her husband. Once again, crocuses peeped through frozen grounds. And along the river-banks, willows

266

turned green and peach blossoms filled the air with fragrance. Except for the occasional company of her sister-in-law, Tse-hung, K'ai-hui was alone, and heavy with her burden.

Early one morning K'ai-hui felt a slight twinge of pain in her back. As she sat by the window, a pair of bluebirds with reddish breast and white belly, flew from one of the trees with hollow limps and settled on the window sills, unafraid of her presence. The shining blue on the birds' backs paled the blueness in the sky. Listening to the camaraderie chirpings that were exchanged between them, she shed little tears for her own missing mate.

"Such a beautiful day for our baby to be born. But you are so far away and I know not where!"

The pain increased until it became almost unbearable.

Calmly she lay a clean sheet on her hard bed. Then she put two clean towels, a clean basin and a bottle of alcohol on the end of her bed. K'ai-hui gently woke her sister-in-law.

"Tse-hung, I think my time has come. Everything is ready."

Tse-hung waited nervously wringing her hands while An-ying ran in and out.

Weak and pale from long hours of labor pains that were now approaching their maximum, K'ai-hui gripped her sister-in-law's hand in seeming desperation.

"How I wish I could fall into a deep sleep," K'ai-hui thought. Evoked by the intensity of the pain and as sudden as summer lightning, a passage from Shakespeare's *Othello* that she read years ago, came to her mind.

> Not poppy, nor mandragor, nor all the drowsy syrups of the world, shall ever medicine thee to that sweet sleep.

She broke out into cold sweat with every agonizing dilation. She did not utter a sound, but only grimaced in pain. Tse-hung, seeing how much her sister-in-law was suffering, said, "Ta Sao[1], I think you need a midwife."

"No, Tse-hung, we must not let anyone know our whereabouts. I'll be fine."

For hours she strained, pushed and sweated, with Tse-hung nervously but courageously urging and coaxing her womb and her muscles to the final orgasmic climax. When finally the small head slipped out, followed by the body, slippery and sleek, K'ai-hui was too exhausted to hear her baby's first cry nor hear her sister-in-law's cry of joy: "Ta Sao, it's a boy! A big healthy boy!"

[1]Wife of eldest brother.

K'ai-hui lay exhausted, a fine tremor shaking her legs and mouth. When Tse-hung put the baby, all wrapped up in one of the towels, in her arms, K'ai-hui wept for hours from joy and sadness.

"Do you think your eldest brother will ever see the baby?" she asked Tse-hung. "Will he ever know Yung-fu is his second son's name?"

K'ai-hui's recovery was slow. Because they had to move to a new hiding place every other day, An-ying was running a fever. Yung-fu, the baby, had diarrhea. They often had to sleep on straw mats on cold damp floors. Their diet consisted of rice gruel and pickled vegetables. But, K'ai-hui was thankful that her supply of milk was plentiful, unaffected by her poor diet. So as she grew thin, her baby kept on growing at the normal rate. She was also thankful to have Tse-hung, her sister-in-law, with her.

"I don't know what I'd do if you weren't here to help me, Tse-hung!" she said.

"You have suffered more than any others, Tao Sao!" Tse-hung replied. "But we might be able to join Ta Ko[1] soon. His forces in Chingkangshan are strengthened by troops led by one from Szechuan called Chu Teh who has just fled from Nanchang. Between them they are forming the Fourth Red Army. Chu is now commander and Ta Ko is political Commissar."

[1]Eldest brother.

269

Despite hardships, knowledge of her husband's safety palliated her personal frustrations.

Patiently she waited for her husband's troops to break through the barricade of Governor Chien Ho's forces in Changsha.

Twice the Fourth Red Army attacked, but both times they were outnumbered and repelled by the much better equipped government forces.

Hopes of their escape from Changsha grew dim. The whole city was under martial law and evening curfews were strictly enforced. Every citizen's movement and activity was being watched. Secret police were everywhere.

"Sooner or later they will ferret us out, Ta Sao!" Tse-hung said sadly. "They'll smoke us out liked hunted animals!"

"Do not despair, Tse-hung! Sooner or later, your eldest brother will think of a way to smuggle us out. He is a clever tactician. He always knows what to do!"

29

Capture

"Fortune and flowers often do not last."
Chinese proverb

CAPTURE

Two comrades came from the Hunan-Kiangsi border, disguised as coolies. One of them was average
in height with fine bronzed skin and good white
teeth. The other was young, very thin, extremely tall
and wiry. He seemed jerky and ill-coordinated. But
his mind was very quick.

The tall one was the first to speak to K'ai-hui and
Tse-hung. "I am comrade Li Lo and my companion
is comrade Chang. We are instructed to be your
porters. You are supposed to be bride and maid
returning to your family for the customary one-
month-after-the-wedding visit. Try to change your
hairstyle or something so you won't be easily identi-
fied."

"The children are to be left here in Changsha
temporarily," the short one said in near perfect
Manderine, with a slight touch of Shensi accent.
"We'll come back for them later on." He then spread
out a map of the countryside and began to brief K'ai-
hui and Tse-hung on the various routes they were to
travel. His speech was fluent, but was constantly
sprinkled with the phase *Wo hai p'a,*-"I am afraid."

273

K'ai-hui listened quietly. She, too, was afraid. "If Comrade Chang is afraid," she thought, "how are Tse-hung and I supposed to feel!" Just when she was going to ask Comrade Chang exactly what it was that he feared, Li said: "Please trust us! Comrade Chang is really very brave. He says 'Wo hai p'a' so much because it is the Shensi colloquialism for 'I don't understand'."

The confidence of Li and Chang put K'ai-hui at ease. The day she lived and hoped for had finally come, yet she was despondent.

She blinked back her tears as her baby was taken away from her breast. At the last minute, she pressed An-ying to her and comforted him. "You and Yung-fu will come to join Mama and Papa soon."

"I'll miss you Mama, but don't worry! I'll take care of Yung-fu while you are gone!" An-ying tried to sound brave.

"You are so loving and brave, my son!" K'ai-hui had to steady her quivering lips.

Cupping his little hands in hers, she did not want him to walk away. A choking grief surged within her, so strong and cutting she thought part of her skin was being ripped away from her body. The road ahead seemed long and empty.

"What if I were never to see them again!" she feared in silence. Suddenly, she turned back to An-ying and drew him to her once more. She hugged him until Tse-hung tapped her on the shoulder saying, "Ta Sao, we must be going now!"

With their forged papers, K'ai-hui, Tse-hung, Li and Chang passed all the government check-points safely. When they finally reached the Kiangsi border, the guard scrutinized their papers for a long time. Then he asked: "Li Lo where are you from?" "Ninghsiang, Funan." Li answered. The guard was satisfied.

"And you, Chang?"

"He's also from Nianghsiang, Funan," Li said.

"Let him answer for himself!" The guard was annoyed.

"Ninghsiang, Hunan." Chang said anxiously.

The guard grew suspicious of Chang's accent. Hunanese almost always say FUNAN instead of Hunan.

"Just one minute! I want you people to step aside for further questioning."

Chang got nervous and the phrase Wo hai p'a occasionally crept in his speech again. The guard became very suspicious and before he could give order to arrest them, K'ai-hui and Tse-hung handed Chang and Li the two pistols they had concealed under their gowns.

Chang silenced the guard with one shot. There was instant confusion in the area and the next thing K'ai-hui knew, she and Tse-hung were running into the mountains with Chang and Li leading the way. They hid in a cave until dusk. Then they heard the shuffling of soldiers' boots. The soldiers were firing wild shots in the air.

When they stopped shooting, one soldier yelled out: "Wherever you are, Mrs. Mao, you'd better come out and surrender. We have your son An-ying here as hostage."

Then the soldiers made An-ying call for her. When she heard her son's voice, she leaped quickly out of her hiding place.

The soldiers killed Chang and wounded Li and Tse-hung. When K'ai-hui tried to cover Chang's bullet-riddled body with leaves, the soldiers kicked and slapped her. Then she, An-ying, Tse-hung and Li were chained and carried off in a cart to the Governor's mansion, like hunted animals.

30

Prisoner at the Governor's Mansion

"Bitter words make good medicine, sweet words carry infection."　　　*Chinese proverb*

PRISONER AT THE GOVERNOR'S MANSION

Upon arrival at Governor Chien Ho's stone mansion, Li was immediately put into a cage where he could only stand. He was bleeding profusely from his gunshot wounds in the stomach.

Tse-hung was allowed to rest and her wound treated.

As for K'ai-hui, not only was she not subjected to physical torture, she received guest privileges by the Governor's orders. She had a large room and her bed was padded with soft silk-covered quilts. Servants were everywhere to attend to her needs. She was served an array of succulent dishes every meal. She was not molested but she felt like one living on an island surrounded by man-eating animals, poisonous snakes and piranhas.

"I don't understand Tse-hung!" she said. "Such good treatment for us! The sly fox Ho is fattening us up for the kill!"

The third day, Governor Ho, whose fabricated kindness did not conceal a habitual snarling temper and cruelty, interrogated K'ai-hui.

"I've been a very patient man, Mrs. Mao. But unless you tell us exactly where your husband's troops are located I shall have to take sterner measures against you. As you know, I've a very highly trained personnel in intelligence work. Just one day after you tried to escape, we managed to locate your sons. We also have very persuasive methods to make people talk."

With an evil laugh, Ho led K'ai-hui to the dungeons, and showed her his torture chamber. It was dark and full of water. Rat-infested, the place stank of human excrement and decayed human flesh.

The majority of prisoners were chained to the floor and wall. "The chains will not be removed until they are dead," Ho said.

The prisoners' clothing had rotted on them. Their hair was long and matted and swarmed with lice. Emaciated skeletons, they looked like wild, terrified animals.

K'ai-hui's heart sank. She was seized with the need to vomit.

"Horrible, isn't it? But I've no choice. These people are my enemies!" Ho's long, horse-like face grew pale and sallow and was so twisted with sadistic pleasure, he looked to K'ai-hui at that moment like one from the lowest level of hell.

"Now, Mrs. Mao, you'll see how we try to persuade your friend Li Lo to talk!"

She could not recognize Li. He was swollen and bleeding from torture.

"A chair for the lady, please! So she can witness our technique comfortably!" Ho said to one of his underlings.

Two men started to question Li Lo. When he refused to talk, they beat him until he fainted. They revived him with cold water. Then the two men went to another room and brought back a long steel chain that was heated to red-hot. They held it in front of Li and said: "Talk!" Li stared at the chain blankly, there was sweat all over his face and he was trembling. Still he said nothing. "Talk! Or else it won't be too comfortable for you if we wrap this chain around you."

K' ai-hui, sick with repulsion and nausea, fainted. When she revived, she cried out, "Please stop! Please stop torturing him. He will talk."

But Li did not talk. Before he expired, he murmured faintly, "Down with all tyrants. I die for all the oppressed people in China!"

That night K' ai-hui could not sleep. When she finally did doze off, she had nightmares and woke up screaming and shaking. Soon she was soaked in cold sweat. Cuddling her sons, one on each side of her, she wept through the night.

There was more interrogation the next day.

"All we want is to find your husband and ask him

to come over to our side. No harm will come to him!" Then looking sideways at K'ai-hui, Ho continued, "By the way, how long has it been since he last wrote you? We have learned through reliable sources that he is living with an eighteen-year-old girl named Ho Tzu-chen who is the renegade daughter of a landlord here in Hunan. She ran away to join the Communists. Apparently she landed right in your husband's bed! Why do you still want to risk your life for a husband who is unfaithful to you?"

"Governor Ho," K'ai-hui replied, "if you know so much about my husband's doings, there's really no need to question me as to his whereabouts. You seem to know a great deal more about him than I do!"

She tried to sound calm but Ho's tittle-tattle jolted her, adding new sorrows to her already heavily burdened heart. She was afraid that she might betray her husband under the pang of jealousy.

She felt her soul squirming in agony of doubts and misgivings. Still, she did not divulge any information Ho sought. She told herself that Comrade Li and thousands of others like him must not suffer and die in vain.

"My patience is running out Mrs. Mao! As you well know, though we do not torture women or children, we have other methods of dealing with them!"

As a drop of water reflects the universe, so did Ho reflect all the virulence of the so-called old Chinese "exquisites" who loved the fragrance of many teas, the euphoria that came with opium, and the suppleness of women's thighs.

"On the other hand, Mrs. Mao, if you cooperate and will persuade your husband to surrender, you'll be on the winning side. I'm a general and have the power to bestow favors on friends and to execute enemies. I would surely hate to hang a beautiful lady like you! As you well know, I am a good Christian. I address the students in missionary schools quite often, telling them to follow the humble teachings of Christ. I urge them to follow the moral teachings of Confucius and forbid them to read any socialist literature."

"Yes, I know," K'ai-hui interrupted, "you drag them out of school and shoot them if you find them reading about socialism!"

"But they are rebels and dangerous!"

"If you are just to the people, Governor Ho, and therefore have their trust, you have nothing to fear. I am sure you are convinced enough of your ideology not to have any fear of a wide-scale rebellion!"

"That will never happen, Mrs. Mao! You see, I take good care of my people. I even look after their spiritual welfare! For the good of their children, I've forbidden the circulation of such books as *Little Red*

283

Riding Hood and *Alice in Wonderland* because if children get the idea that animals can talk, they will be unable to see the difference between human beings and animals!"

"I don't think we have to worry about that too much Governor! I am sure children will have no difficulty in distinguishing human beings from animals. The former bicker and kill for greed and self-aggrandizement, the latter, only for survival."

K' ai-hui's remark pinched a nerve. Ho's face turned purple, he was smoldering with rage. Pounding the table with his fist, he shouted. "Enough! You have till tomorrow to make up your mind. If by then you still resist, you'll be put in solitary confinement. After that . . ." Ho stopped short, cursed and walked away.

K' ai-hui shuddered. Later that day she talked to Tse-hung. "There's no telling what Ho will do to us!"

"His inhuman behavior is a sad testament to his own fear and suspicion," Tse-hung said. "He feels threatened by Ta Ko and so we are in great danger."

"Whatever happens we must never betray your eldest brother, Tse-hung!"

All through the night the wind seemed to howl and scream like spirits calling from another world. Although her children were sleeping soundly beside her, she felt alone and was assailed by a miserable glumness. All at once her maternal feelings welled up, and the chill in her stomach grew to fear as she pondered the possibility of a permanent separation from her children. Lost in the fathomless gloom, she was unable to rise out of it.

She caressed her sons' cheeks and careful not to wake them, kissed them gently on their foreheads. "My sons! My dear An-ying and Yung-fu, who's to take care of you if I should have to die!"

She found herself unable to accept death, even though she had been taught to accept it as the only sure thing in human existence. The finality of death and the thought of leaving her children motherless plunged her into an abyss of despair.

K'ai-hui lived the next few days in solitary confinement. Overcome by a fever of anxiety, she was so lonely and worried about her children that she could neither sleep nor eat. She had no idea where Tse-hung and her children were, or what Ho was going to do with her.

"Just pull this bell on the door if you decide to cooperate," one of Ho's servants told her.

"How about my children? Am I never to see them?" K'ai-hui went on her knees before the servant, who seemed kind and sympathetic. "Please I must see them lest I go mad with grief!" Touched by K'ai-hui's suffering, the servant helped her to bed.

Still dizzy from longing and grief, she felt a terrible pang, as for something vital lost. The mood which began her every day would last the whole day through.

Her hand went to her breast to soften the pain where the milk gushed still. It was warm and stuffy in her tiny room, but her body was shivering with cold. Somewhere in the courtyard she heard a baby's hungry cry. But when she glanced out she found the courtyard empty, save for a few sentries on duty. She saw An-ying walking towards her, but when she reached out to touch him, he was not there.

"An-ying! An-ying!" She called and found her hand reaching for the string to pull the bell on the door.

Then she was gazing into the blood-stained face of Li Lo and heard the painful cry of prisoners under torture in the prison next to her shack. Somehow her mind had also slipped back. She saw the empty stares of starving children. She saw blood oozing slowly from the peasant woman's wounded breasts. The peasant woman was pleading: "Lord Master, have mercy! I steal only because my baby is starving!"

Then the face of her husband appeared. A loving and compassionate face. He was taking his cotton jacket off and putting it on the shoulder of the bare-breasted peasant woman.

She collapsed and fell on the floor before her hand could reach the bell. After a few hours of rest, her mind became clear. Her heart convulsed with revolutionary zeal and simultaneously, it blazed with compassion for all those who were oppressed. She was filled with a greater love, beyond that of a mother for her children, and she vowed to fight and to resist even if it meant loneliness and death.

She tried to forget the present and dream of a world that once was hers. To bolster her downtrodden spirit, she recited in her mind poems she had learned when she was a teenager.

A SOLDIER'S WIFE TO HER HUSBAND

If it is your duty to
    die for your country
And to the dust on
    the far north frontier you must return,
Know
That my feelings for you will be
    strong and imperishable
Like that stone
Upon the mountain side.

Liu Chi
Ming Dynasty

[1] From Chinese Love Poems. Edited by D.J. Kelmer, illustrated by Seong Moy. New York, Hanover House, 1959

She tried to remember poems written by ancient emperor-warriors which told of brave warriors and of battles won despite hardships. K'ai-hui thought of her husband as one who would be a leader among leaders in the tradition of poet warriors, the pre-eminent hero of his age. As his wife and companion, she was impressed by his earnestness and by his willingness to sacrifice personal longings and comfort in the pursuit of an ideal. Like herself, his spirit dwelt within himself, isolating him from the masses, except for the few who were closest to him.

She thought of their courting days and was glad to be reminded of the intricate passion and lasting nature of their love.

"Even if he lives with another," she thought, "his heart will always belong to me. It took us almost ten years to reach that most secret depth in each other, that stage far deeper than emotion or passion, where reason and instinct are in accord. He might betray me in body, but never in his heart!"

It was not her habit to doubt her husband and she thought it odd that she should suddenly place such weight on Ho's unfounded remark. But how could Ho have known so much about Ho Tzu-chen? That Ho Tzu-chen is tall and beautiful and had one time been a student at Changsha First Normal College.

"He will always be faithful!" K'ai-hui reassured herself.

288

Turning from the present, she abandoned herself completely to reveries. When she tried to shape the future after her own fancy, there was all about her an air of solitude, of nature depopulated, of vast emptiness stretched into nothingness, of death, and of the negation of death.

She would not be able to love and care for An-ying and Yung-fu; to see them grow; to praise and to console them; to hold them close to her bosom. They would cry for her and she would not be there. In death she would exit into the dark cold earth below never to return.

Death, she thought, could be as heavy as Mountain Tai or light as a feather, just as Confucius had said.

31

Dreaming of a Far-away Wife

"Far waters cannot quench near fires."
                                    Chinese proverb

DREAMING OF A FAR-AWAY WIFE

It was drizzling when Mao arrived at the foot of Ching-kang Mountain whose sharp peaks were shrouded by heavy clouds. He had just returned from another successful battle against the Nationalist troops.

In centipedal files, soldiers and women squeezed themselves through narrow passages and treacherous ravines.

Mao heard the swish of his bare feet on the wet earth which was soothing to his aching, bleeding soles. The murmur of his companions' voice as they poured through the dark ravines sounded to him like the distant incoming tide of the sea.

A voice startled him. He looked around but could see nothing. The voice echoed: "Pass word please, Comrades!"

When Mao gave the appropriate pass words, soldiers began emerging from the drifting rain clouds behind rocks, from clefts, from behind bushes on the mountain cliffs. These peasant soldiers, swinging over rocks and ravines with lithe, ferocious swiftness, led Mao's regiment through winding secret passages to one of the mountain peaks where thousands of new recruits, young men and women, sat in rapt attention, waiting for Mao to make a welcoming speech.

For some of the new recruits, the first impression of their hero was one of disappointment. The man they had heard so much about and whom they admired was perhaps more ideal in their imagination than in the flesh.

At first Mao spoke as though his mouth were full of hot congee, and his voice did not carry well. He expressed himself in short, clipped, simple sentences, but slowly and with many pauses. Though not particularly gifted in public speaking, his ability to use vivid metaphors often lifted his listeners to great heights. His ability to speak in this hard factual manner endeared him to workers and peasants. At times he was humorous and satirical, and at times, forceful and crude. When expounding on the writing of Marx and Lenin, he simplified it to layman terms, for the benefit of all present.

After his speech, he shook hands with the new soldiers who found his handshake limp. He neither grasped nor shook their hands. Rather, taking theirs into his, he sort of pushed them away.

While carrying on a lively discussion with his soldiers, Mao lighted a cigarette and sucked in the smoke with an unpleasant noise. He smoked his cigarette to the very last bit until he almost burned his fingers holding it. He lighted another one almost immediately. He was continually blowing smoke like a chimney!

He wore a crumpled tunic, the right breast pocket of which was unbuttoned and the collar points unrestrained. His trousers were ripped at the cuffs. His socks were so full of holes that his big toes stuck out of his sandals. His hair, a trifle too long, and parted in the middle, hung carelessly in tufts over his ears.

Those close to him were not ruffled by his manners and his lack of concern with personal appearance. They were used to his many curious habits. He had been known to absent-mindedly turn down the belt of his trousers and search for lice, or to take off his trousers on a hot day in the presence of visitors. It was easy for his comrades to overlook any number of faults for his one enduring virtue, his total dedication to his cause.

That night, Mao slept very little. News from Changsha was discouraging. There were rumors that Ho Chien was still holding K'ai-hui and Tse-hung prisoners, though he had freed the children An-ying and Yung-fu.

Mao worried about their safety. "There's no telling what the tyrannical Ho would do!" Mao shuddered.

Unable to fall asleep, he sat up in bed and began to work frantically on the progress report that he would soon deliver as the secretary of the Special Committee in Kiangsi. He had to put his personal feelings aside so he could concentrate on matters of national importance.

When he finally went to bed in his clothes, Mao dreamed that K'ai-hui was safe with him in Kiangsi. They were roaming the cliffs of Chingkangshan. K'ai-hui was so happy she danced beside him, and spring was bright green all around them.

She spread her arms and said: "Everything is beautiful here, I wonder why you took so long to bring me here, Tse-tung!" She then began to cry as she talked, pressing her handkerchief against her lips. He watched her coldly, hating her for crying. "When you cry, K'ai-hui, it's because you think there is no hope for us or for China! If you think that, then you ought not to be here!" K'ai-hui wiped her eyes. "But Tse-tung," she said, "I am your wife, and I haven't seen you now for nearly a year!"

"We are having a hard time, K'ai-hui. Everybody in China is having a hard time. We must sacrifice our own happiness for the good of our country!"

Mao awoke the next day with a heavy heart.

32

Death by Execution

*"We come to earth bearing nothing; we go to death
bearing nothing."*   *Chinese proverb*

DEATH BY EXECUTION

For weeks K'ai-hui was not allowed to see her children or to move around in her tiny cell. For food she had thin rice porridge with the merest pinch of salt. Her stomach ached from pangs of hunger.

Sandwiched between the luxurious mansion and the dilapidated prison, she smelt odors and heard noises of great contrast. From one side blew fragrances of fresh food and the sweet smell of cleanliness, from the other, decaying garbage. From one side drifted the symphony of pleasant voices, of wine glasses clinking, of satisfying giggles, culminated after lustful frolicking; from the other, screams and the slow moaning of dying prisoners. She was indeed living between heaven and hell.

For days now she heard workmen busy at work erecting a scaffold in the courtyard. Their banging and pounding penetrated every tired bone in her body. Gripped with fear, she also looked forward to the peaceful sleep, rest at last for her tired mind and body.

The next day they came for her. After she was washed and bathed, she was served a three-course

meal of meat, rice and vegetables. So long deprived
of decent food, she could not even swallow. She had
been kept sitting for so long that her legs were weak.
She wobbled and trembled. Away from the sun for
months, her eyes blinded and watered when she was
led by two soldiers to the scaffold.

Sensations of triumph and defeat, spasms of heat
and cold, passed incessantly through her mind and
body.

She saw Tse-hung being led by two other soldiers,
coming to the other side of the scaffold. Formerly a
big and robust girl, Tse-hung was now skin and
bone, a walking skeleton.

Putting her body's whole strength behind her,
K'ai-hui called, "Tse-hung!" But Tse-hung only
stared at her with darting eyes, expressionless and
empty.

An-ying, walking behind one of Ho's servants
who was holding Yung-Fu, came toward her. At the
sight of her two sons, sorrow regurgitated pain that
crept from the feet up. The time it took her to walk to
her children seemed like an eternity.

She wanted to stretch out her hands to receive
them, but her hands were bound tightly behind. A
soldier untied her and she quickly drew both of her
children to her bosom. She embraced them and
wished with agony that she had hugged them more

when they were together. Tears streamed down her cheeks forming two rivulets alongside her nose.

Yung-fu was still too young to understand. He just howled from fright. An-ying hugged her so tight that he put marks on her neck. His little chest heaved and he was sobbing like a baby, tears streaming down his face. Their loud sobs interrupted the heavy silence that brooded over them.

K'ai-hui ran her hands down An-ying's hair, took his hands and pressed them to her cheeks. She must tell him that she truly loved him even though she was going away forever. But no words came.

She wanted to tell him his favorite story. She wanted to sing him his favorite lullaby. She wanted to comfort him. She wanted to measure and weigh him to see how much he had grown. But there was no time. How she wanted to immobilize time at that moment, to eternalize ephemera!

When the soldiers tore An-ying away from her, he was still crying and saying, "Please don't kill Mama! Please don't hang her! She is good! She has not done anything bad! I love my Mama! Please don't . . ."

She strained to look at her children who were being led away through the crowd. The last she saw of them, Yung-fu had stopped howling but An-ying was still crying and wiping his tears with the palm of his hands.

Her head whirled, her forehead throbbed. She wept, her body trembling and her legs racked with cramp. She was choked with grief from this final parting and her throat went raw. She felt numb as if part of her were already dead.

The flow of recollections paraded in her mind again. The faces of her parents, her husband and her sons appeared before her in rapid succession as though they were mounted on a drum which kept going around and around.

She saw a handsome young man with sensual lips and a prominant mole on his chin smiling at her.

"Tse-tung!" She breathed his name.

She wanted to shout to the crowd: "Tse-tung will come to liberate all of you someday!" But no words came out of her quivering lips.

She looked around silently with darting eyes, and now there was no thought. Her confused mind remembered not her sons, not her husband, but only a chilling sensation of loneliness. She desperately wanted to hold onto someone so that she might warm her trembling hands. But the crowd was silent. No one moved toward her.

Somewhere in the valley a bugle sounded. It played a monotonous, melancholic tune that sank deep into her.

"Tse-tung!" she whispered. "Tse-tung!" and a choking painful agony filled her whole being. Inside her a faint voice cried, "Your proud Poplar lonely, lonely, lonely . . ."

The crowd shrank back, farther and farther and still farther until they were non-existent before her. Closing her eyes, she floated lightly away into total darkness.

33

A Lonely Man Mourns

"The Yangtze does not flow backwards and man re-captures not his youth."   *Chinese proverb*

A LONELY MAN MOURNS

Mao was snoring when his orderly shook him awake at noon. "Commissar Mao," the orderly said, "they are waiting in the Assembly Hall for you to give a speech."

Mao got dressed quickly and gulped down a bowl of hot congee, his first meal of a two-meal day. Before he went out, his orderly reminded him: "Commissar, how about your notes?"

"I don't need them," Mao replied, "I think I know what I want to say."

Men, women, and children, all dressed in the same simple garb—cotton trousers and tunics, shirts or blouses of blue, grey, khaki, black, or white, had filed into the room. Soon the immense lecture hall was filled to capacity.

Mao looked around and saw familiar faces among thousands of unfamiliar ones, all half hidden under the soldiers' caps with the red star. In this sea of moving caps and dancing red stars, Mao felt lonely and lost.

He heard whispers, even giggles, as he, gaunt, tall, massive, and in his usual baggy tunic and crumpled trousers, walked awkwardly to the center of the stage. He still looked and acted like the peasant he was, and somewhat of a school teacher he had become—easygoing and simple. Before he began, he cleared his throat and blew his nose.

"Comrades: I am happy to report that we have six border districts under our control since the first Soviet Government was set up in Tsalin, on the Hunan-Kiangsi border a little more than two years ago," he began slowly.

"Now we have more than 1000 cooperatives in Kiangsi alone. Our strategy for the next year, in opposition to recommendation of some Party members, is to try to stabilize and consolidate our power in the Hunan-Kiangsi-Kwangtung border districts. From these bases we can then expand to other areas.

"There are some among us though, who believe struggle of the peasant masses must be closely linked to the revolutionary struggle of the urban proletariat, 'proletarian hegemony' remains their dogma. They not only advocate the leading role of the urban proletariat in this revolution, they also want to narrow the class basis of the Communist Party. Furthermore, they also want to plan an all-or-nothing campaign in the near future to recapture cities rapidly rather than expanding the 'Red Areas' in the countryside gradually until the entire country is engulfed.

"Comrade Chu Teh and I have different opinions. We believe that these base areas, not cities, are essential if we are to succeed. We must shoot with aim. But some comrades shoot with meaningless words and fancy, imported theories. Without practical experience, they do the revolution a great deal of harm.

"Our country is vast, chaotic and lacks adequate means of communication. Therefore, we need not take all the country at once. Instead, it is better to set up armed bases in the hills, at the border of two provinces where the sphere of influence of different warlords overlaps. A warlord's strength decreases as he leaves his capital.

I am convinced that a base area bears the same relation to an army as does the buttock to a person. Without either, one can neither rest nor recuperate, but will be forced to run about until exhausted or defeated!"

The audience laughed and applauded enthusiastically. While the hall rang with laughter, Mao stood with his eyes lowered, silent, contemplating.

"How reserved he is," Mao's orderly observed, "I have yet to see him smile in public!"

Mao again cleared his throat and wiped his brows. He continued: "In recent weeks, the Kuomintang (Nationalist) armies have been mounting new offensives against all our bases, especially this one here.

"Next week, Comrade Chu Teh and I will move

southeast into southern Kiangsi. Some of you will come with us. But Comrades P'eng Teh-huai and Wang Tso and their men will remain here in Chingkangshan.

"We are outnumbered in men and weapons, but so far, we have successfully evaded our enemies, who can only fire at random in our rear. When overpowered by men with superior weapons, we cannot fight a conventional war. We must not crash head on with our enemies. Instead, we must retreat when our enemies are strong. Then attack when they are weak. In other words, we must fight a guerrilla war.

"It will be bloody because revolution is not a dinner party, not a literary composition, nor a painting, nor a piece of pretty embroidery. It cannot be carried out softly, gradually, carefully, considerately, respectfully, politely, plainly, modestly. Some of us will lose sons, daughters, wives, parents, brothers, sisters and friends. But everyone of us must fight with high spirit.

"Everyone of us must be imbued and fight with a sense of purpose. But most important of all, we must have the support and trust of the common people in our land. We must never loot or plunder. We must live among them like fish in the water. Then, no amount of currents, however fierce, will ever toss us out of this turbulent sea that is our country today!"

310

He thanked the audience for coming, bowed, picked up a pile of books near the podium and hurriedly walked away, before the audience had the chance to break into applause.

Just then, a soldier, carrying a bundle, walked hastily towards Mao as he was leaving the Assembly Hall.

The soldier said solemnly: "Commissar Mao, we just heard words from Changsha that comrades Yang K'ai-hui and Mao Tse-hung were executed by Ho Chien last week. An-ying and Yung-fu are safe. Comrade Yang's head was hung over the city gate for three days to serve as warnings for other revolutionaries!" Then giving Mao the bundle that he was carrying, the soldier added: "Our guerrilla soldiers found Comrade Yang's belongings in an abandoned cave. What are we to do now, Commissar? Shall we attack Changsha again to teach that tyrant Ho a lesson?"

"No comrade," Mao replied sternly, "we'll proceed as planned." As he gave his orders, Mao's heart pounded fiercely and he felt numb. Without saying another word to the soldier, he hastened away.

He must have walked on for a mile until he came to a tree behind a large rock. He sat down and rubbed his nose and cheeks on the bark. The roughness and pain felt good. He lay back in the

311

shade and looked through the leaves to the sky. He would wait before he conferred with his comrades. And when he did, he hoped everything would be all right. Some other messenger would come to tell him: "Commissar, we were mistaken, K'ai-hui and Tse-hung are not dead!"

"I just saw her last night in my dreams," Mao argued in his thought, "nothing so terrible as death could have happened between midnight and noon!"

He lay there for a long time until the sun sank lazily in the western horizon. His mind was blank most of the time.

So it was true. K'ai-hui was dead, hunted, imprisoned, and executed.

Mao walked. He took out a photograph of her and stared at it. He wondered if she had tied her hair with a red ribbon as she often would when she was with him. He tried to remember the things she had done . . . The way she smiled at him the first time he saw her at her home in Changsha. . . The graceful movement of her fingers when she was pouring tea . . . The way she threw back her head when she laughed . . .

When he was alone that night, time hung heavily. Upon him there descended a loneliness devoid of all human feelings, rather like the time when his

312

mother's coffin had been lowered below the ground and the dirt was being shovelled back into the grave.

"At such time," he thought, "one needs some sort of remembrance." He searched through his simple belongings, a big brief case that was full of documents and a bundle that contained another change of clothing. He searched through the pages of his books and something fell out of one of them. He picked it up. It was a letter that he had written months ago to K'ai-hui but had never sent. Blankly he stared at the letter, and sadness filled his whole being. "Oh K'ai-hui," he murmured, "it must be hard for you. All these months and not one word from me!" He was at once assailed by remorse as he wondered how he had been able to leave K'ai-hui and An-ying behind!

Numbly he untied the bundle that the soldiers had found in the cave. A pair of his wife's shoes, quite old and worn, was wrapped in a newspaper. He picked them up and ran his hand inside them to feel the ridges that her toes had made. He turned them over to look at the soles. There were two holes in the right one next to the heel. He rewrapped the shoes neatly before he unfolded her clothes, one article at a time, and put them on his bed. Then he buried his face among them. The clothes still carried her scent.

Like a portrait artist who seeks to immortalize his subject, Mao drew in his mind the portraits of two

313

young people—his wife, K'ai-hui with her fair skin, delicate face, and clear eyes; and his sister, Tse-hung, with her charming mouth and tilted eyes set in a pleasingly plump face. And he cried in his heart: "No matter what, K'ai-hui, I shall always love you. In my thoughts I have never left you. Though I was always away I was with you always!"

Her delicate face, her gentle smile were all still vivid in his mind. But her soul came and went like the wind, eluding his embrace. She was in heaven and he on earth. But their oneness had not been separated completely.

"We must be bleeding from the same wound in two different worlds, K'ai-hui!" Mao whispered. "Forgive me, my Poplar!" And he wished he had told her more often that he loved her and no other. A strong wind sprang up, and together with the clearness of the stars, created an impression of coldness as if winter had suddenly returned this summer night.

Mao closed the shutters and sat staring vacantly at the flickering candle, wax dripping down like tears.

BIBLIOGRAPHY

Books and articles consulted

Archer, Jules
  Mao Tse-tung. New York, Hawthorn, 1972

Bain, Chester A.
  The Far East, by Chester A. Bain, edited by Helmut G. Callis, third edition. Paterson, New Jersey, Littlefield, Adams and Co., 1961

Barnstone, Willis
  The Poems of Mao Tse-tung. Translation, introduction, notes by Willis Barnstone in collaboration with Ko Ching-po. New York, Harper and Row, 1972

Birch, Cyril, ed.
  Chinese Communist Literature. New York, Frederick A. Praeger, 1963

Blakney, R. B.
  The Way of Life: Lao Tzu. A new translation of the Tao-Te Ching, New York, New American Library, 1955

Bloodworth, Dennis
  The Chinese Looking Glass. A Delta Book. New York, Dell Publishing Co., 1967

Boorman, Howard L.
  "Mao Tse-tung: The Lacquered Image." The China Quarterly, no. 16 (Oct.-Dec., 1963)

Brandt, Conrad, Schwartz, Benjamin and Fairbank, John K.
A Documentary History of Chinese Communism. Cambridge, Mass., Harvard University Press, 1952

Ch' en, Jerome, ed.
Great Lives Observed: Mao. Englewood Cliffs, N.J. Prentice-Hall, Inc., 1969

Chung, Hua-min, and Miller, Arthur C.
Madame Mao: a Profile of Chiang Ch'ing. Kowloon, Hong Kong. Union Research Institute, 1958

Elegant, Robert S.
China's Red Masters: Political Biographies of the Chinese Communist Leaders. New York, Twayne Publishers, 1951

Elegant, Robert S.
The Center of the World: Communism and the mind of China. New York, Doubleday, 1964

Fairbank, John K.
China: The People's Middle Kingdom and the U.S.A. Cambridge, Mass., Harvard University Press, 1967

Fessler, Loren
Life World Library by Loren Fessler and the Editors of Life. New York Time Inc. 1963

Gardner, Charles Sidney, Comp.

A Union List of Selected Western Books on China in American Libraries, second edition, revised and enlarged. (American Council of Learned Societies, Committee on Chinese Studies, Washington, D.C., 1938) New York, Lenox Hill Publishing, 1972

Han, Suyin

Destination, Chung King. Boston, Little Brown, 1942

Hsiao, Yu

Mao Tse-tung and I Were Beggars. New York, Syracuse University Press, 1959

Hughes, E. R.

The Invasion of China by the Western World. London, Black, 1937

Malraux, Andre

Anti-memoirs. Translated by Terence Kilmartin. First American edition. New York, Holt Rhinehart and Winston, 1968

Marcuse, Jacques

The Peking Papers; Leaves from the Notebook of a China Correspondent, First edition, New York, Dutton, 1967

The New York Times

Report from Red China. New York, Avon Publishers of Bard, Camelot, Discus and Equinox Books, 1972

317

Paloczi-Horvath, George
Mao Tse-tung: Emperor of the Blue Ants. First edition in the U.S.A. Garden City, New York, Doubleday, 1963

Payne, Robert
Mao Tse-tung, Ruler of Red China, London, 1951

Pelissier, Roger
The Awakening of China 1793-1949 edited and translated by Martin Kieffer. New York, Putnam's Sons. First American edition, 1967

Rice, Edward E.
Mao's Way. Berkeley, California, Univ. of California Press, 1972

Roy, Jules
Journey through China. Translated from the French by Francis Price. First U.S. edition. New York, Harper and Row, 1967

Schram, Stuart R.
Mao Tse-tung. New York, Simon and Schuster, 1966

Schwartz, Benjamin J.
Chinese Communism and the rise of Mao. Cambridge, Mass., Harvard University Press, 1951

Shih, Bernadette P. N. Lee, and Snyder, Richard L., Comp.
International Union List of Communist Chinese serials. Cambridge, Mass., Massachusetts Institute of Technology Libraries, Aug. 1963

Smedley, Agnes
China Fights Back. New York, Vanguard, 1938

China's Red Army Marches. New York, Vanguard, 1934

Smith, Arthur H.
Village Life in China. New York, Revell, 1899

Snow, Edgar
Battle for Asia. New York, Random House, 1941

The Other Side of the River: Red China Today. New York, Random House, 1961

Random notes on Red China 1936-1945. Cambridge, Mass., East Asian Research Center, Harvard University, 1968

Red Star Over China. Rev. ed., New York, Grove Press, 1968

Strong, Anna Louise
   The Chinese Conquer China. New York, Doubleday, 1949

Taylor, Charles
   Reporter in Red China. New York, Random
   House, 1966

Terrill, Ross
   800,000,000 The Real China. Boston, Little Brown,
   1971

Trumbull, Robert, Ed.
   This is Communist China, by the staff of Yomiuri
   Shimbun, Tokyo. New York, McKay, 1968

White, T. H., and Jacoby, Annalee
   Thunder out of China. New York, Sloane, 1946

Williams, Maslyn
   The East is Red; the View inside China. New
   York, W. Morrow, 1967

Wilson, Dick
   The Long March 1935: The Epic of Chinese
   Communism's Survival. New York, Viking, 1971